The Wahine Di

– *A Tragedy Remembered* –

Emmanuel Makarios

*The majestic bow looks powerful and sleek
towering above the crowd of shipyard workers
and guests gathering for the launch day.*
Museum of Wellington City & Sea

Grantham House Publishing
in association with the
Wellington Museums Trust

Dedicated to the people who lost their lives in the Wahine disaster and to all those whose lives were touched by the events of 10 April 1968.

The powerful looking Wahine *on sea trials before being handed over to the Union Steam Ship Company of NZ Ltd.* Museum of Wellington City & Sea

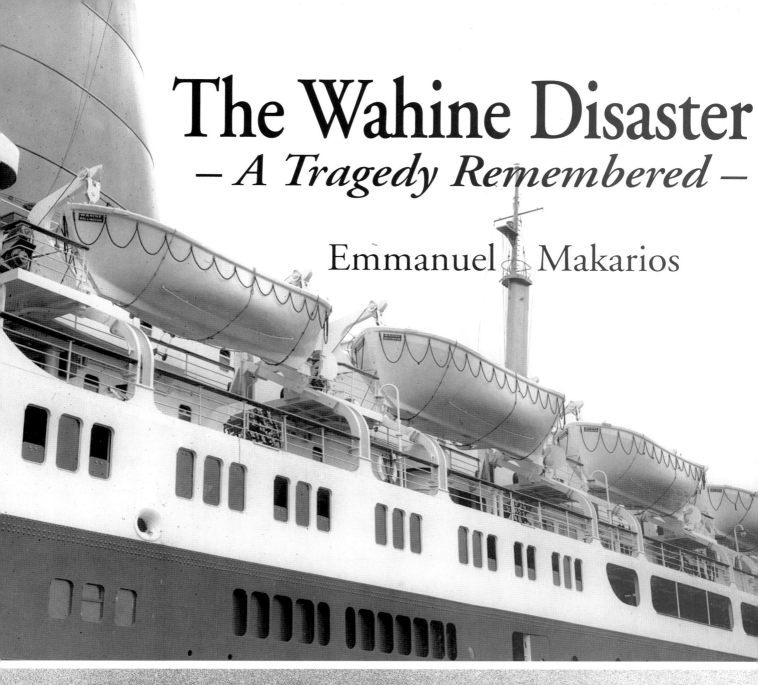

The Wahine Disaster
– *A Tragedy Remembered* –

Emmanuel Makarios

The Wahine's death roll. Many people looked on, stunned, as the once proud steamer express vessel began to roll over and sink. **Dominion and Sunday Times**

The Wahine *nears the launch stage at the builder's yard in Glasgow. The vessel's name can be seen on the side towards the stern.* Museum of Wellington City & Sea

Facing page: The Wahine *enters Wellington Harbour. Pencarrow Head is in the background.*

Below: The Wahine *launching ceremony – "I name this ship Wahine, may God bless her and all who sail in her." Mrs MacFarlane, wife of the Union Steam Ship Company of New Zealand Limited, managing director, performs the honours as a strike of the gavel releases the customary bottle of champagne against the bow.* Museum of Wellington City & Sea

Shipyard workers observe the awesome sight of the Wahine *sliding down the ways into the water.* Museum of Wellington City & Sea

Preface

My interest in the Wahine stems back to late March in 1968 when I travelled on the ferry with my Standard Four class from Berhampore School in Wellington. Being a young boy with a passion for things Maritime, travelling on this big beautiful new ferry left a real impression on me.

Two weeks later I would be woken in the morning by a howling wind and heavy rain. As the morning progressed our small house in Berhampore was shaken by the terrible wind as it strengthened. Looking towards Kingston we could see roofing iron flying through the air and as a family sitting in front of our transistor radio listening to the reports of damage happening around our city and the shocking events that were unfolding out in the harbour.

Some years later I went to sea in the New Zealand Merchant Navy as a seaman and sailed on ships with some of the ill-fated Wahine crew. Naturally I was interested in learning more about their experiences but none would be forthcoming with their memories of that day. Being young I guess I didn't fully appreciate just what these people went through. As time has gone by some people have been more comfortable in relaying their experiences. Years later I have been very privileged through my work in firstly the Wellington Maritime Museum and later the Museum of Wellington City & Sea, in meeting survivors and crew which has helped me to appreciate their ordeal. Also one of my duties for a number of years was to talk to school groups and other visitors to the museum about the Wahine Disaster.

All these experiences have prompted me to put together this book which whilst not being easy reading, I hope that for those of us who remember that terrible day may help us to respectfully remember that time and for those who do not know anything about the disaster I hope this snapshot of one of New Zealand's worst Maritime disasters will help them to understand the trauma that was felt.

Emmanuel Makarios

A graceful yet powerful looking vessel, the Wahine *speeds along on her sea trials.* Museum of Wellington City & Sea

Below: *Part of an advertising brochure from the 1960s.* Museum of Wellington City & Sea

THE WORLD'S FINEST OVERNIGHT SEA-CROSSING

Half the pleasure of getting there is travelling by Steamer Express between Wellington and Lyttelton. Worry-free travel for families and holiday-makers, no waste time for business men. A fast modern ship is your overnight "hotel". You arrive relaxed, refreshed, and on time. Nightly sailings (except Sundays) from Wellington and Lyttelton (port for Christchurch); additional sailings during Summer holiday period.
T.E.V. "WAHINE" 9,000 TONS
T.E.V. "MAORI" 7,480 TONS

TAKE YOUR CAR WITH YOU
Both "Wahine" and "Maori" provide up to the minute Drive-On facilities for large numbers of cars and caravans. Passengers with cars may report at any time up to 7 p.m. No tedious delay on arrival. Drive off a few minutes after your ship berths. It's as simple as garaging your car overnight. For added convenience, toll tickets for the Lyttelton–Christchurch road tunnel may be obtained at the Purser's office on board.

FOR UNSURPASSED INTER-ISLAND TRAVEL CONSULT:

UNION STEAM SHIP COMPANY OF NEW ZEALAND LIMITED
or AUTHORISED AGENT:

2 Berth Cabin

Below: *A passenger ticket issued for an overnight passage from Lyttelton to Wellington on the T.E.V.* Wahine *on 21 September 1967. The cost was $8.50.* Museum of Wellington City & Sea

MAORI

C474.

UNION STEAM SHIP COMPANY OF N.Z. LTD.

STEAMER EXPRESS DRIVE-ON SERVICE

WELLINGTON
LYTTELTON

LYTTELTON
WELLINGTON

PASSAGE TICKET

WAHINE

Late afternoon, twilight and night scenes at Lyttelton of the Wahine *as the ferry express steamer prepared for a night sailing from Lyttelton to Wellington.* Museum of Wellington City & Sea

your highway for tonight?

T.E.V. MAORI

PORTION OF SMOKEROOM (WAHINE)

2 BED CABIN WITH FACILITIES

CORNER OF LOUNGE (WAHINE)

BOOK HERE!
for the STEAMER EXPRESS DRIVE-ON SERVICE
Wellington-Lyttelton ★ Lyttelton-Wellington

"WAHINE" (8944 tons) and "MAORI" (7480 tons) MAINTAIN A REGULAR SERVICE BETWEEN WELLINGTON AND LYTTELTON AND PROVIDE COMFORTABLE ACCOMMODATION FOR PASSENGERS AND FULL DRIVE-ON SERVICE FOR CARS, CARAVANS, AND TRAILERS.

UNION STEAM SHIP CO. OF N.Z. LTD.

A striking colour poster used in booking offices throughout New Zealand. Museum of Wellington City & Sea

The main vehicle deck. More than 200 vehicles could be transported on the ferry, including cars, trailers, and caravans. Heavy machinery like earth moving and other heavy trade vehicles could be transported along with unitised cargo carried in containers, seafreighters, and on cargo trays. Museum of Wellington City & Sea

The cafeteria (aft end of rear of A-Deck) – a very functional and modern interior design with bright colours. Museum of Wellington City & Sea

The general lounge. For an overnight ferry, the passenger accommodation was of a very high standard. Museum of Wellington City & Sea

The Smoke Room – the passenger bar is situated behind the formica screens. Many of the passengers assembled here on the morning of 10 April 1968, awaiting further instructions. Museum of Wellington City & Sea

A very comfortable and highly functional two berth cabin on C deck. The Wahine was fitted with one, two, three, four and twelve-berth cabins, consecutively over six decks. Few had shower and toilet facilities. However, all were fitted with electric shaver connections and a wash-basin with a hot and a cold water supply. Museum of Wellington City & Sea

Introduction

The Wahine *arrives at the Wellington Overseas Passenger Terminal after the delivery voyage from the United Kingdom, welcomed by an enthusiastic crowd.* V H Young & L A Sawyer collection

On the morning of 10 April 1968, Wellingtonians awoke to gale force winds and torrential rain. Most people greeted this as an indication that winter was around the corner. However, by the time they had begun to leave home for work or school, conditions had dramatically worsened. Roofs were being stripped off houses and trees blown over. Power lines toppled and a number of small commercial and pleasure craft were swept off their moorings and washed ashore.

Out in Cook Strait, the steamer express ferry *Wahine* was making her way from Lyttelton to Wellington on the regular overnight service. On board were 123 officers and 610 passengers, plus two stowaways. The latter, seamen Len Cord and Laurie Sayers, were intending to join the crew of the rail ferry *Aramoana* in Wellington. This unofficial manner of travel, not uncommon among seamen, was dubbed "sailing as a ringbolt."

The passage from Lyttelton had thus far been uneventful. Although the weather conditions were rough, the ship was behaving well, as she was running before the rough sea. Given that a south-south-westerly of 35-45 knots was blowing, the passengers were not too uncomfortable. At 4.00 am the bridge log recorded conditions as "overcast with continuing heavy rain, rough sea, moderate to heavy swell, moderate visibility, vessel rolling heavily at times, pitching and scending at times." Such conditions, not at all unusual for Cook Strait at any time of year, would not normally have posed any problems for the *Wahine*.

This large, state of the art vessel was relatively new and the jewel in the crown of the Union Steam Ship Company's Wellington-Lyttelton passenger service. At 8,944 gross registered tons, she was the largest roll-on roll-off passenger ferry of her kind, and the first purpose built ro-ro ferry for the steamer express service. Fitted with accommodation for 123 officers and crew and 928 passengers, she was a twin screw vessel powered by a turbo-electric propulsion system. Her service speed was 17 knots, but she was capable of a maximum service speed of 21.7 knots if required to make up time. At 148.74 metres long and 21.64 metres wide, the *Wahine* was a similar size to the *Arahura* and *Aratere,* which operate on the Inter-Island service between Wellington and Picton more than 30 years later.

Conscious that the roll-on roll-off type ferry was the way of the future, the Union Steam Ship Company had, in January 1964, awarded the contract to build the vessel to the Fairfield Shipbuilding and Engineering Company Limited of Glasgow, Scotland. From the outset however, the process had been plagued by industrial problems and labour shortages plus financial troubles ultimally causing the company to be put into receivership. It was only through the intervention of the British government that a new company, Fairfields Glasgow Ltd, was raised from the ashes and the ferry completed.

The *Wahine* was launched with the traditional bottle of champagne in July 1965 and finally fitted out, completed and handed over on 18 June 1966. She was in fact the second Union Steam Ship Company vessel so named. The first *Wahine*, built in 1913, had served with distinction in both world wars. After working the Wellington-Lyttelton run for many years, she was wrecked in 1951 carrying troops to the Korean War.

Unlike her predecessor, however, the new *Wahine* had a short career. On 10 April 1968 the ferry foundered at the entrance to Wellington Harbour in a severe southerly storm, with a loss of 51 lives. The disaster devastated New Zealand and sent shock waves around the world. The following account draws on archival and secondary sources and on the recollections of people who survived that terrible journey.

The Chairman of Directors of
Union Steam Ship Company of New Zealand Ltd.
Mr. F. K. Macfarlane and Captain E. G. K. Meatyard

invite

to cocktails on board t.e.v. "Wahine" to mark the entry of
this new drive-on vessel into the Lyttelton/Wellington Steamer Express Service.

R.S.V.P.
Telephone 65-019
Miss Sillars

Place: T.E.V. "Wahine".
Date: 2nd August, 1966
Time: 4.00 p.m. to 6.00 p.m.

Please present this invitation at the gangway.

The Union Steam Ship Company celebrated the commissioning of the Wahine *on the Lyttelton–Wellington steamer express service with an on-board cocktail party on 2 August 1966.* Museum of Wellington City & Sea

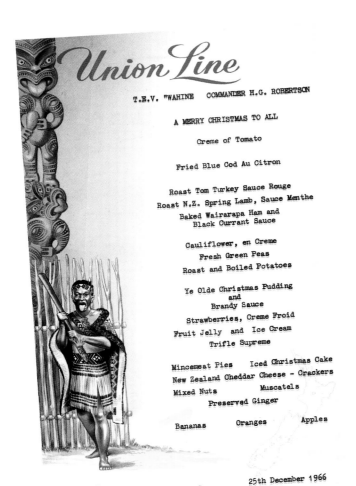

The Wahine *had only been in service for four months when the crew celebrated their first Christmas Day on board with Captain Robertson in command.* Museum of Wellington City & Sea

The forward passenger entrance boasted this mural entitled Wahine, *which is the Maori word for woman. This mural is now on display in the Museum of Wellington City & Sea.*

Gale or Storm Force

The previous evening the *Wahine* had received a weather forecast stating that strong northerly winds would change to southerlies after midnight and become gale or storm force about Cook Strait during the morning of 10 April. These conditions were due to a severe tropical depression, which had its origins in the Coral Sea, close to the Solomon Islands. On 6 April the depression had developed into tropical cyclone Giselle which was moving to the south and thought to be weakening. The weakening cyclone was now approaching the top of the North Island of New Zealand, but as it got closer to land it started to gain strength. On 9 April the Meteorological Office reported that conditions were favourable for the tropical cyclone to regenerate into a mid-latitude depression of unusual intensity.

On 9 April the effects of the mid-latitude depression had started to make an impact on the north of the North Island. Heavy rain and winds gusting 86 knots per hour were experienced at Cape Reinga. A Kaitaia farmer attempting to secure a pile of hay bales had been blown off the bales in a fatal accident. Houses in the surrounding district were surrounded by flood water. The unexpected ferocity of the weather caught many by surprise. While bad weather had been expected, no one had imagined the conditions would be so dire.

On Ninety Mile Beach two busloads of tourists were stranded due to the worsening storm. On the east coast at the Bay of Islands a number of pleasure craft were blown ashore. Many areas were flooded, with thousands of hectares being submerged. Land slips blocked several roads. By midnight, the storm's centre was off Great Barrier Island. Auckland was now feeling its effects, with heavy rain and very strong winds causing a number of houses to lose roofs.

Earlier in the evening of 9 April, the Meteorological Service had expected that the storm would travel down the North Island in a south, south easterly direction. But with such a severe depression it was difficult to be exact, and contrary to expectations it began, to alter course and speed up. In the early hours of 10 April the storm roared into the Coromandel Peninsula sending two commercial fishing vessels ashore and wrecking havoc in the area. Out at sea the *Masa Maru*, a Japanese log carrier, had developed a moderate list due to her cargo shifting in the extreme weather conditions, and headed for shelter.

At 3.00 am on 10 April the storm was buffeting Tauranga. The sea was so rough that in some areas along the coast waves were making their way up the shore into the pastures. Farm buildings and houses lost their roofs or were blown over. As the storm continued on its course down the North Island it tore off more roofs, including part of the Whakatane hospital. More fishing vessels and pleasure craft were wrecked. At Waiotahi 81 hectres of coastal farm land were under sea water due to storm surge. Many farm animals were drowned or survived only by seeking whatever high ground they could find. St Mary's Church at Opotiki lost its steeple and its structure was badly strained. A number of fishing and pleasure craft were swept across roads and into paddocks. Trees, power and phone lines were blown down, making many roads and railway lines impassable.

Napier was next: Marine Parade felt the storm's force as many of the buildings had their windows blown in. Hasting's orchards had the fruit stripped from the trees. Wanganui, Rangitikei and the Manawatu were also devastated. Pine forests were badly affected with many trees being blown over. Then the storm made its presence felt in the Wellington area.

Storm warnings had been issued as it was expected that conditions within 300 nautical miles of the New Zealand coast including Cook Strait, would be gale or storm force. The weather report was passed on to the *Wahine*'s master, Captain Hector Gordon Robertson, who noted the situation, but expected his ship to be safe in her berth before the worst of the weather made its presence felt. On 9 April the *Wahine* departed Lyttelton at 8.43 pm, instead of 8.00pm, due to the delayed arrival of the connecting rail service from Invercargill. This was a common occurrence but the ferry had ample reserve power to make up any lost time. Since entering service the *Wahine* had always been punctual, arriving on schedule at 7.00 am.

At the time of departure a 15 knot south-westerly had been blowing. Once clear of the inner harbour, the *Wahine* made her way down Lyttelton Harbour towards the entrance. At 9.05 pm she reached Godley Head and Captain Robertson altered course to take the vessel up the East Coast of the South Island towards Wellington. All this time the weather conditions steadily deteriorated.

As night moved on, the mid-latitude depression, which had been travelling at 20 knots, increased its speed to 25 knots and altered course. From midnight to 9.00 am it would travel 300 nautical miles, leaving a trail of destruction in its path as it moved down the island. It became one of the worst recorded storms in New Zealand's history.

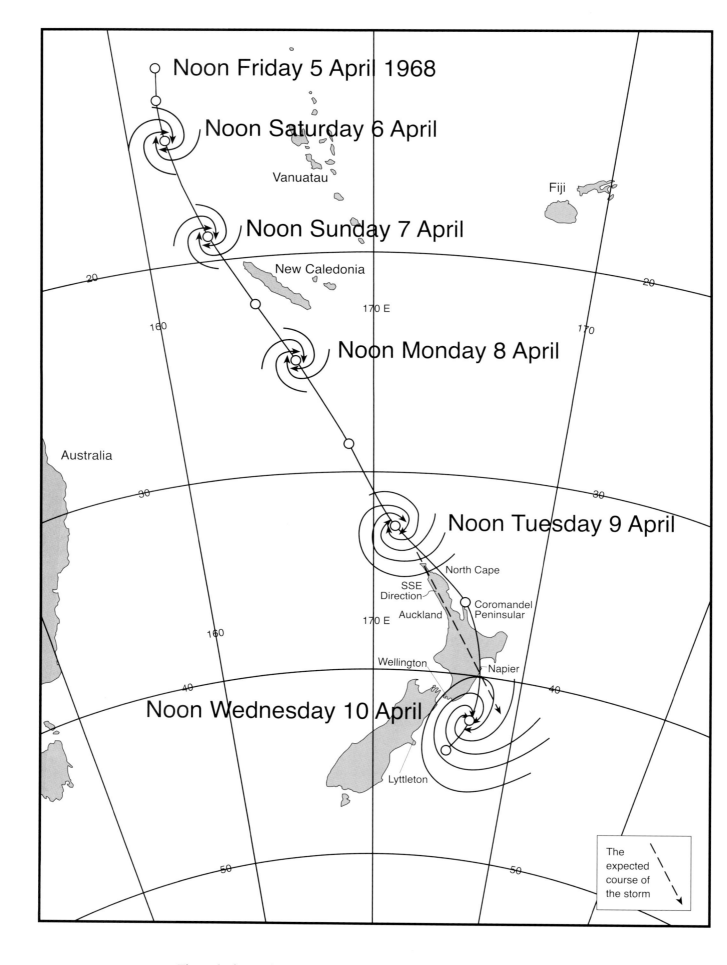

The track of tropical cyclone Giselle as it approached New Zealand, which
became a mid-latitude depression as it neared North Cape. MetService

This brochure was issued by the Union Steam Ship Company to advertise the roll-on – roll-off service when the steamer express ferry Wahine *joined the service. Her partner, the* Maori, *had been converted to a roll-on – roll-off vessel in 1965.*
Museum of Wellington City & Sea

T.E.V. "WAHINE" – WORLD'S LARGEST ROLL-ON / ROLL-OFF VESSEL

The regular two-way service operating daily, except Sundays, with "Wahine" and "Maori" GUARANTEES overnight delivery in Wellington and Lyttelton, and at the same time eliminates the risk of transit damage to goods.

UNION STEAM SHIP CO. STEAMER EXPRESS SERVICE

* LOWER FREIGHTS
* SPEEDY DELIVERY
* DEPENDABILITY
* FREEDOM FROM DAMAGE
* REGULARITY OF SERVICE

The operation of these two vessels brings about the effective marriage of sea and road transport and makes available the latest cargo handling methods to shippers in the Wellington and Christchurch areas.

This speedy and safe service can be recommended with confidence, and the Company looks forward to co-operating with shippers and Road Transport Operators in meeting their most exacting requirements.

Approaching Safe Harbour

Back on the *Wahine*, crew and passengers were preparing for their imminent arrival at Wellington, with no warning of what was unfolding. As the *Wahine* was crossing Cook Strait the ship's barometer fell 5.6 hPa (hectopascals) or 5.6 millibars in one hour and 15 minutes. The wind and sea conditions were also worsening.

Seventeen year old deck boy Alan Windsor was one of the youngest crew members. Filling in for the regular deck boy, who was on leave, he had only been on the *Wahine* a matter of weeks. In his short time at sea, Alan had been employed on a variety of cargo ships. But the *Wahine* was his first ferry; the largest, most modern vessel he had worked on to date. That morning Alan, whose workday started at 6.00 am, rose at 5.30 am and enjoyed a cup of tea with a fellow seaman on the poop deck at the ship's stern before it reached the heads. He noticed how dark the sky seemed as they looked towards the south, but the sea conditions were not unusually rough. The wind, though strong, was typical of a Wellington southerly.

After returning to the seamen's mess room Alan went to raise the New Zealand ensign at the stern, his first duty of the day. Going out on deck he quickly realised that the wind conditions had increased considerably, making it difficult for him to stand. Hauling the flag up the ensign staff was impossible so he gave up, thinking he would do it once the ship was in the shelter of the harbour. Back in the mess room again, where the seamen ate their meals and received their orders, he and several others were told to go down to the vehicle deck to check on the cargo as the ship's movement had increased. After checking the cargo, they decided extra lashings should be attached to some of the large vehicles. Normally at this time they would have been preparing to remove the lashings from the cargo.

As the ship made her approach towards the harbour entrance the chief officer, Rodney Luly, who was on watch, was informed that a tug would be available to assist the *Wahine* into her berth, if required, due to the weather conditions. Captain Robertson, when he arrived on the bridge to take the ship into port, noted that the

The Wahine on the Jubilee Floating Dock, Wellington, for an annual survey, one year before tragedy struck. Before the order was given to abandon ship on 10 April 1968, many people, both on board and ashore, believed that by the end of the day she would be safely back on the dock for repairs. Brian Smith

sea was rough and had a considerable swell. He estimated the wind to be 40-50 knots.

He then checked the ship's course and line on the leading lights, which help guide ships into harbour, also looking to see the ship's position on the radar. All was in order. At 6.00 am the ferry passed Baring Head, now only 15 minutes from entering the harbour. It was around this time conditions started to rapidly deteriorate as the fury of the storm travelling off Napier began to be felt both in Wellington and on board the *Wahine*.

Next the ferry passed Pencarrow Head, which was abeam at 6.10 am. Conditions continued to rapidly worsen. With visibility limited, the master put the main engines on stand-by and reduced speed to half ahead. It was at this crucial time that the ship's radar failed and a number of other incidents followed which ultimately caused the loss of the *Wahine*.

The vessel suddenly began to broach to port, swinging off course by 23 degrees. In an attempt to stop the swing and bring the *Wahine* back on course towards the harbour, the helm was put hard to starboard. The ship did not respond. Captain Robertson ordered full ahead on both engines to give the vessel more forward momentum to help with steerage. But at that moment the ship rolled very heavily to starboard, throwing all personnel except the helmsman off their feet. Captain Robertson was flung the full length of the bridge, striking the radar console on the way. Badly shaken, he quickly pulled himself together and ordered full astern on the port engine to assist the ship in the turn to port, which had already begun when she broached.

The sudden broach had caused mayhem down on the vehicle deck as well as on the bridge. The crew were flung violently about, with most losing their balance and falling. Extra lashing had just been added to a truck loaded with coke and now all the lashings snapped as if they were string. The truck toppled onto its side, spilling its cargo over the deck. This loose coke later contributed to the *Wahine*'s loss. Other vehicles and cargo also fell because of the extreme rolling. With vehicles and cargo sliding around the deck, the seamen took shelter wherever they could. Alan and several others sheltered behind a portable vehicle ramp which gave them some protection. After securing what they could they decided it would be safer to return to the mess room and check for further orders. Elsewhere in the ship, passengers and crew got to their feet after having been flung about by the sudden roll. Down in the engine room, personnel had also been thrown about during the horrifying event.

The Maori and the Wahine at the old Wellington inter-island wharf on Sunday 16 April 1967. The Wahine had just completed an annual survey and re-entered service the next day. H. Jauncey Studio

A Precarious Position

The Wahine was now in a very precarious position as the ship was close to the rocks of the Pencarrow coast to the east and nearby Barrett Reef on the west. The propellers and rudders were out of the water as much as they were in, giving the master very poor control of the ship. Captain Robertson endeavoured to get the ferry under control and manoeuvre her back out to the relative safety of the open sea where she could ride out the storm. In the course of these manoeuvres (in almost zero visibility) the Wahine was either flung onto or struck a submerged pinnacle rock adjacent to the Outer Rock, the southernmost rock of Barrett Reef. The initial impact was on the ship's starboard quarter. This severed the starboard propeller and part of the propeller shaft, which allowed water to enter the engine room. After a few minutes power was also lost on the port engine, leaving the ferry without propulsion. She was at the mercy of the wind, and seas

The Wahine *off Steeple Rock, as seen from Seatoun – at this stage the ship was riding the waves well and was quite upright. It was hoped if the weather conditions improved a tug could tow the* Wahine *into calmer waters. However, when the wind eased, the tide dropped very rapidly and the sudden outpouring of pent-up water caused the* Wahine *to swing and take on a heavy list.* Evening Post

that were growing stronger and larger.

The seamen making their way back to the mess room had just reached its door when the dark shape of a rock rose into view out of the murk. They could only stand watching as ship and rock collided. Alan Windsor recalls a horrendous noise of steel grating against rock and the propeller striking the submerged reef at full speed. The vibration was felt throughout the ship but particularly strongly here. As each huge wave passed under the *Wahine* it brought the ship crashing down on to the reef, inflicting more damage. It was like a nightmare in slow motion.

When the Wahine *made initial contact with Barrett Reef the propeller was severed. It is shown here, broken and twisted, at Queen's Wharf after being removed from the wreck.* Evening Post

Below: The Wahine *was a twin screw and twin rudder vessel. This photograph was taken when the* Wahine *had her last survey in the Wellington floating dock in April 1967. The propeller on the right broke off when the ship struck Barrett Reef.* E. Beck

Down in the engine room sirens were sounding as the watertight doors slid shut. Earlier, Chief Engineer Herbert Wareing and his five engineers and two electricians, had worked frantically to respond to the captain's telegraph orders as he tried to manoeuvre the ship back out to sea. When the ship struck, the shudder

An emergency water-tight door in the Wahine *engine room. One of many such heavy metal doors throughout the ship; it slid across the opening and could be automatically closed from the Bridge.* Museum of Wellington City & Sea

and vibration in the engine room on the ship's lowest level was extreme. One of the engineers informed Wareing that water was flooding into the motor room towards the stern of the ship. The bridge was advised and the emergency pumps were started. The chief engineer inspected the motor room by going up to the vehicle deck and peering through an engine room casing door. The water was almost to the top of the deckhead (ceiling). Concerned about the weight of the water on the bulkhead (wall), Wareing returned to the engine room but found the bulkhead was holding up.

All watertight doors were closed and passengers and crew were instructed to go to their cabins and put on their lifejackets. Passengers were then mustered on B deck to await developments. Some of the providore staff assisted them with their lifejackets. Others were placed around the accommodation areas to make sure passengers did not wander away from the muster stations back to their cabins. The chief steward, Raymond Gifford, and second steward Bryan McMaster, made a thorough inspection of the passenger accommodation, checking each cabin to ensure it was empty.

At 6.42 am, Wellington Radio ZLW received a message from the *Wahine* stating, 'Going ashore think near the heads'. At 6.50 am Beacon Hill Signal Station on the western side of the harbour entrance, which monitors shipping arrivals and departures, received a radio message from the ferry which stated 'Our position is Barrett Reef'. The wind and sea were now pushing the *Wahine* along and across the reef causing serious hull damage.

Captain Robertson ordered Chief Officer Luly, and the bosun George Hampson, to release the anchors, not an easy task under the circumstances. As the two men struggled towards the forecastle where the anchors lay, Captain Robertson watched their progress from the bridge. Both men were now crawling on their stomachs

'ringbolts' presented themselves to Captain Robertson and offered to go to work with the *Wahine*'s crew, which was readily accepted.

In an attempt to gauge how much the *Wahine* had settled in the water, Captain Robertson stood on the starboard wing of the bridge watching the huge seas sweep down the side of the ship, hoping to see something that might help him plan his next move. By this time the ship had worked its way clear of the reef. The anchors were down but it took some time for them to get a hold. Although they were dragging, the anchors held the stricken vessel's bow towards the oncoming waves and wind. This enabled the vessel to better ride over the waves.

After dropping the anchors the captain had ordered the chief officer to prepare the lifesaving equipment in case it was needed. This involved dragging some of the liferafts, which were stored under deck seating, to the side of the ship and securing them there, ready to be inflated should the need arise. This was extremely difficult for the seamen as the fierce wind, heavy rain and the rolling and pitching of the ship made keeping their footing precarious. Some lifejackets stored in lockers

along the deck towards the anchor windlass. Robertson saw the bosun suddenly picked up by the wind and flung against the ship's rails. With great difficulty they finally reached the windlass. To let the anchors go they had to lift two compressers (heavy steel bars which go across the anchor cable to help secure the anchors). Then the two devil's claws, a bottle screw arrangement, had to be unscrewed and removed from the cables, after which the brakes had to be unscrewed before the anchors could be released. Even in good conditions this was a time consuming procedure. It took half an hour to accomplish something that would normally have taken ten minutes.

Around this time, the two seamen travelling as

The terrifying conditions encountered are graphically shown in this photograph taken from the deck of the Wahine, *with the tug* Tapuhi *in the distance.* David Hendy

on deck were also readied. A number of these were the only ones available for persons under 32 kilos. While working on deck the chief officer was under no illusion as to what would happen to all on board if it had been necessary to abandon ship at that particular moment. At the Court of Inquiry he stated conditions were so bad "that everyone aboard would have washed ashore dead, whether or not they had a lifejacket on."

After preparing the liferafts, Luly was then ordered to inspect the vessel for obvious damage and report to the captain. The inspection included the vessel's stern door, which was found watertight. Further inspection found flooding in the steering motor compartment, extensive flooding on F deck and in numerous other compartments. As Luly worked his way along the vehicle deck he found a mess of vehicles, seafreighters (containers), spilt cargo and other large and small objects which had broken their lashings due to the terrible conditions when the *Wahine* broached. Some of the cargo had shifted, spilling coke and eggs over the deck. This concoction would cause some of the emergency scuppers (drains) on the vehicle deck to become blocked, ultimately preventing seawater flooding onto the vehicle deck from being discharged overboard. Seamen had now returned to the vehicle deck to clear doorways of

An engineer takes a photograph of the water on the Wahine *vehicle deck. This water would cause the* Wahine *to lose stability, roll over and eventually sink.* F.T. Robinson

Whilst making his way to the B deck muster station, David Hendy took this photograph of fellow passengers in one of the ship's alleyways on B deck. David Hendy

Below: *The* Wahine *crew prepare rocket firing gear to send a line across to the tug* Tapuhi *in an attempt to get a towing wire on-board the* Wahine. *The Steeple Rock light can be seen through the mist.* F. T. Robinson

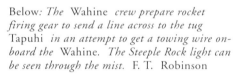

obstacles and secure anything that was still moving about.

Later, Luly nearly lost his life when he and able seaman Dennis O'Reilly were making an inspection of a compartment on the foc'scle head (the deck at the front of the ship). Luly was caught by the wind and blown against the railing but O'Reilly caught him before he was blown overboard.

On returning to the bridge the chief officer made his report to the captain. Due to the extent of the flooding they assumed that the double bottom tanks were damaged and estimated that 3,000 tons of water were aboard. Though the *Wahine* had lost some of her buoyancy she was still rolling and coming back to vertical in a positive manner, indicating sufficient stability. Rather than risk pumping water out and possibly upsetting this stability it was decided to concentrate on keeping the remaining compartments dry.

In a cheerful frame of mind – A steward talking to two young women passengers while waiting instructions – still hopeful that everything will be alright. F. T. Robinson

Concerned for the engine room staff, Robertson ordered them to evacuate the engine room in case they got trapped below. Before leaving, the engineers shut down the boilers then made their way to A deck to await further orders. They later returned to their duties.

When the *Wahine* finally cleared Barrett Reef it looked as though she would go ashore at Point Dorset on the western side of the harbour entrance, as she was swinging wildly around on her anchors. Captain Robertson had already alerted Beacon Hill Signal Station, when, miraculously, the *Wahine* cleared the point and drifted further into the harbour. Earlier, another harbour pilot, Captain Peter Mitchell, was sent to Fort Dorset with rocket lifesaving apparatus and a portable VHF radio in case the ship had gone ashore. Had the vessel gone aground at Point Dorset there would very likely have been

Ordinary Seaman Alan Windsor, December 1968, on board the cargo ship Waikare. *Windsor, who served as deck boy aboard the* Wahine, *was determined not to let the traumatic experience affect a seafaring future.* A. Windsor

a greater loss of life. The *Wahine* drifted close to Steeple Rock light, approximately half a kilometre off Seatoun Beach and the suburb of Seatoun.

It was at this time that the vessel's anchors took hold. The *Wahine* was still sheering about but she was upright and still afloat, giving those aboard and ashore confidence that she could ride out the storm until towed to safety.

Now that the *Wahine* was riding her anchors and inside the harbour, Alan and the other seamen felt that the immediate danger was over. Alan Windsor went up to the bridge to see what was happening and saw Captain Robertson and others appearing calm and confident, although they carried out their duties with an air of urgency.

A rock at Barrett Reef emerges out of the raging sea as the Wahine, *now with no engine power, drifts helplessly towards the harbour entrance.* David Hendy

Below left: *In the* Wahine *accommodation area, Sharon Major, with baby Sarah, appears calm. When the ferry was abandoned, Sharon and Sarah were put into a liferaft and later rescued by a tug.* F.T. Robinson
Below: *They eventually landed safely at the Inter-island Wharf. Having survived the events of 10 April, Sarah later enjoyed a successful career in the world of professional dance.* Evening Post

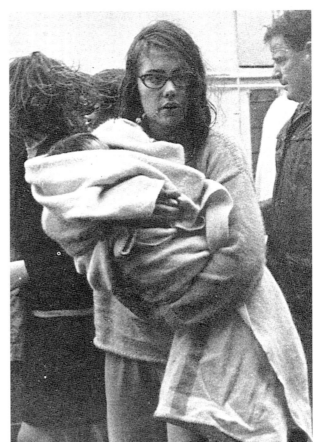

A Nervous Wait

Left: *Women and children wait in the* Wahine *public room after the ship had struck Barrett Reef.* F. T. Robinson

Passengers were sitting where they could find space, some smiling and talking nervously to each other. Others sat quietly, deep in their own thoughts, anxious about what might develop and trying not to show their fear as the sound of the storm raged around the ship.

Among these passengers was a Welshman, David Hendy, who was in New Zealand on a working holiday. His time in the country was coming to an end as he was travelling to Wellington to join the passenger liner *Southern Cross* to travel on to South Africa. The previous evening he had enjoyed a few beers and some conversation with other passengers, but the bar was closed early due to the predicted bad weather so he retired to his cabin for the night. He first knew that the *Wahine* was in trouble when a steward told him to get some warm clothes on, grab his lifejacket and get up to B deck. Once dressed, he put on his lifejacket and picked up his camera, leaving behind his cheque book, passport and cash.

The providore staff did their best to reassure the passengers and provided them with food and hot drinks, though the latter were now only lukewarm. Many of the passengers found it funny seeing their fellow travellers sitting around in the public rooms wearing the bulky and uncomfortable lifejackets. As the public rooms could not accommodate all the passengers some sat in cabins or in the alleyways (corridors on B and C decks). Many people were suffering from seasickness due to the ship's motion. Stewards handed out blankets as by now the ship had no heating.

Gazing out a window David strained his eyes to see any signs of the nearby shoreline and looking down at the boiling sea he could make out the rocks of Barrett Reef. Grabbing his camera he ran along the deck towards the cafeteria to try and get a better view. On reaching the cafeteria he took a photograph of a rock near the ship. One of the stewards offered him some sandwiches and a cup of tea and, sitting there among his fellow passengers wearing lifejackets, David felt reasonably calm.

Over the public address system, passengers were reassured that the ship was in no immediate danger as it was drifting into the harbour. Most accepted this, unaware of the full extent of the damage and the danger to the *Wahine* . To many it seemed impossible that such a large, modern ship could really be in danger of sinking.

One of the passengers mustered in the smoke room was Shirley Hick with three of her children, David Knight, aged six; Alma Hick, three, and Gordon Hick, whose first birthday was that very day. Shirley had travelled to Lyttelton on 8 April with her four children. On that occasion her eldest son Peter, aged seven, had been travelling with them. Peter had a hearing disability and Shirley was taking him to Christchurch to a school in Sumner which specialised in educating children with hearing disorders. The trip down from Wellington had been a good one. The group was only staying in Christchurch for the day, and after settling Peter into school, Shirley and the three other children would return on the *Wahine* that night on their way home to Shannon. As they were going ashore two stewards suggested that as

Shirley Hick holding baby Gordon, with son David in the smoke room. F. T. Robinson

the weather that night was supposed to deteriorate it might be a good idea to settle the children down early. During the day the weather had been wet in Christchurch so the family returned to Lyttelton early in order to board as soon as possible.

The family went straight to their four berth cabin on D deck. After a busy day the children were tired. Shirley recalls that David and Gordon went happily to bed, but Alma was overtired and took some time to settle. Once the children had gone to sleep Shirley went up on deck to watch as the ship departed from Lyttelton. The last of the cargo was still being loaded and there was a short delay before sailing. Once clear of the harbour the *Wahine* started to feel the effects of the southerly wind. Shirley didn't sleep well as she was pregnant and easily woken by the ship's movement and the creaking bulkheads. About 5.30 am she got up and began to get the children ready for the arrival in Wellington. She was taking Alma to the toilet when she heard and felt the ship grind into something: the *Wahine* had struck Barrett Reef. Startled, she returned to the cabin as other passengers emerged, wondering what had happened.

Once back in the cabin she heard an announcement over the public address system asking passengers to take their lifejackets and make their way to the muster stations in the ship's public rooms. Stewards moved through the accommodation making sure that passengers had heard the announcement and were following instructions. They also helped people put on their lifejackets and reassured them that everything would be all right.

Shirley struggled to keep a cool head for her children's sake, despite her own fear. As she was gathering the children, the cabin door opened and a steward entered to offer his assistance. He took Alma; Shirley carried Gordon and a passenger from a cabin opposite took David. They slowly made their way along the now congested alleyways toward the smoke room. As they walked they suddenly realised that they could no longer hear the ship's engines and that the lights had dimmed. There was also a smell of diesel oil which had escaped from the ruptured fuel tanks. Shortly afterward another announcement was made warning people not to smoke or light matches.

As the crowd of passengers arrived at the smoke room, Shirley found a place for herself and the children. Sitting nearby was Dianne Houltham, a young woman travelling alone and visibly upset. On seeing Shirley's hands were full, she offered to help and took Alma. She gathered some of the other young children and entertained them with songs, trying to distract them (and herself) from what was happening.

Outside the wind continued to shriek and mountainous waves swept past the ship. Many people chose not to look out the windows because of the terrifyingly huge waves. One of the passengers had a small transistor radio over which they listened to news of the destruction ashore. Shirley and some of the others felt that somehow they were safer than those ashore who were in danger from loose roofs and hurtling debris.

In the aftermath of the disaster, the captain would be criticised for not keeping the passengers more informed about what was happening. He later stated, 'It is no good rushing around shouting out orders, it panics people right down to the deck boy'. If the crew had had to deal with panicked passengers on top of everything else, there would almost certainly have been more deaths and injuries. At that time it was more important to maintain calm, particularly as the ship was in no immediate danger of sinking, being still upright and stable. Any attempt at abandoning ship would have been suicide at this stage as the lifeboats would have capsized before they got clear of their falls (wire ropes which lower the boat to the water).

A Distressed City

By 9.00 am on 10 April the centre of the storm was passing the eastern entrance to Cook Strait, only 60 to 80 nautical miles from Wellington. At this time the capital experienced its strongest winds, with 78-98 knots being recorded at the airport. The strongest gust - 145 knots - ever recorded in New Zealand was on top of a cliff at Oteranga Bay on the shore of Cook Strait, a few miles to the west of Wellington.

The city was reeling from the impact of the storm, with some of the hillside suburbs suffering terrible damage. The worst affected were the houses on the south coast, and the suburbs of Kingston, Karori and Northland. Huge waves surged over the coast road and onto properties. Winds were gusting well in excess of 100 knots and roofs were peeled off houses as if they were built of playing cards. Some houses sustained serious damage and others were totally destroyed.

Kingston was one of the city's newest suburbs and still under development. It suffered some of the worst damage on shore that day and resembled a war zone. Many residents had to be evacuated. Houses shook with the force of the wind as if they were experiencing an earthquake. Trees were being uprooted and carried some distance away and the sound of the wind was terrifying.

Emergency vehicles were doing their best to get around the city but many streets were blocked by slips, fallen trees and toppled powerlines. One ambulance had to be abandoned at Houghton Bay on the city's south coast. When it was recovered after the storm the side of the vehicle facing the sea was sandblasted down to the bare metal and covered in dents from flying stones.

Wellington and Hutt hospitals were also feeling the effects of the storm. Their casualty departments were dealing with a large number of minor injuries. As the morning progressed more seriously injured people arrived with severe head injuries caused by flying debris or falling trees. In Northland a young girl was killed when a piece of debris blew through her bedroom window. Both hospitals were operating on emergency power. At Hutt Hospital the operating theatres were unusable due to flooding. Police had alerted Wellington Hospital to the *Wahine*'s situation around mid-morning and warned of potential casualties. The hospital was put on general alert. Both hospitals would be further tested later that day.

Kingston, Wellington - an unknown photographer captures the horrendous weather conditions. Kingston was one of the worst affected suburbs in the city. Alexander Turnbull Library (Reference EP/1968/1556-F)

Kingston Heights, Wellington. This type of storm damage has rarely been seen in New Zealand. Alexander Turnbull Library (Reference EP/1968/1580-F)

High Street, Island Bay - a house is severely damaged due to the fierce winds that struck the south coast. Alexander Turnbull Library (Reference EP/1968/2014-F)

The section of road between Lyall Bay and Houghton Bay on Wellington's south coast. Due to the extreme wind, cars overturned and other vehicles were abandoned. Alexander Turnbull Library (Reference EP/1968/1581-F)

While fighting its way to Seatoun the tug Tapuhi *ended up with nearly a metre of water in its engine room, as water made its way down through ventilators and less than watertight doorways. Severe wind sent the harbour tug out of control on three occasions. Ultimately it could do little to save the* Wahine, *but through excellent ship handling the crew were able to rescue survivors from the water and life-rafts. They saved a total of 174 people. This photograph, taken from the* Wahine, *shows the* Tapuhi *manouvering into position to get a tow wire aboard the stricken ferry.* David Hendy

To Assist a Distressed Vessel

As these events were happening out in the harbour Captain John Brown, a harbour pilot employed by the Wellington Harbour Board, was on his way to work. He had been woken by a call from Beacon Hill because he had an early job. While preparing to leave his Johnsonville home he could not help but notice the stormy conditions as his back fence had been blown over. Driving down Ngauranga Gorge into the city his car was buffeted by severe gusts of wind. Captain Brown began to doubt that his early job (shifting a cargo ship from one berth to another) could go ahead. After arriving at Queen's Wharf, he radioed the ship's master to postpone the shift. He also notified the Union Steam Ship Company tug *Tapuhi*, which had been scheduled to assist, at the same time suggesting to the tug's master, Captain Athol Olsen, that he should stand by to assist the *Wahine* into her berth. He then waited in the Deputy Harbour Master's office, reading the morning paper and waiting for other staff to start work at 8 am.

While there he heard the *Wahine* call Beacon Hill with news of their predicament. Captain Brown rushed to call the Harbour Master, Captain Ralph E Suckling,

but couldn't get through. He then telephoned Captain William Galloway, the Deputy Harbour Master. Captain Galloway instructed him to prepare the launch *Tiakina* for sea and to meet him at Seatoun Wharf where Galloway would come aboard. He also told Captain Brown to get the *Tapuhi* back to the wharf so the large rope fender around the vessel's bow could be removed. The rope fender is used as a cushion between the tug and the vessel it is manoeuvring. With heavy seas to go through, Galloway thought it was better removed.

The watch foreman was told to get the *Tiakina's* crew on board ready to go. At about 6.55 am the *Tiakina*, under the command of Captain Brown, departed Queen's Wharf and made its way towards Seatoun. While in Lambton Harbour and in the shelter of Mt Victoria, conditions did not seem that bad. However, on clearing

Captain Athol Olsen on the forward deck of the tug Tapuhi. *Though he and Captain Cyril Sword handled the* Tapuhi *admirably on 10 April 1968, she was unable to operate successfully in the horrendous sea conditions.* Museum of Wellington City & Sea

The pilot launch Tiakina *off the stern of the* Wahine. *This launch played an important rescue role. However, because she sat high out of the water, reaching survivors proved very difficult.* David Hendy

Point Jerningham and steaming across the mouth of Evans Bay, Captain Brown and his crew started to appreciate the strength of the storm. 60-80 knot winds from the south were buffeting the 24.38 metre launch and visibility was down to only a few metres, with heavy rain and two to three metre waves. Still the launch crew were not yet concerned for their own safety. Lack of visibility was the main concern but as *Tiakina* was equipped with radar the master relied on this to reach Seatoun safely. Though it was now daylight, visibility was only about five metres due to the very rough sea, spindrift and heavy rain.

At about 8.05 am the *Tiakina* arrived at Seatoun, taking about 40 minutes longer than normal. Captain Galloway was waiting on the wharf and as the pilot launch came in, he jumped aboard. The launch continued towards Steeple Rock and the harbour entrance. Weather conditions continued to worsen. As the *Tiakina* rounded Steeple Rock Beacon, Galloway and Brown could just make out the *Wahine* south of them near Chaffers Passage on their radar. Captain Galloway asked John Brown to try and get closer to the stricken ferry, but with visibility now zero they were unable to see the seven to eight metre breaking waves. After only making about 100 metres they withdrew to the relative shelter of Worser Bay near Seatoun. The wind was shrieking and visibility in the bay was about 15 metres. Captain Galloway called the *Wahine* on the radio and was informed both her anchors had been dropped. It was believed that the ship could ride out the storm.

Back at Queen's Wharf, the Harbour Master, Captain

Suckling, had ordered his staff to prepare to assist the distressed vessel. Another harbour pilot, Captain Cyril Sword, a very experienced ship handler with a sound knowledge of the harbour, was ordered to join the tug *Tapuhi* . Captain Brown considered Sword to be the best of the pilots when it came to ship handling.

Captain John Brown, on the rail ferry Aratika, *after leaving the Harbour Board. On 10 April 1968 Brown's excellent pilot skills and ship handling abilities enabled him to steer the pilot launch* Tiakina *close enough to the* Wahine *to let Captain Galloway leap onto a lifeboat ladder.* Museum of Wellington City & Sea

Poor Visibility and Dangerous Conditions

Both the *Tiakina* and the *Tapuhi* had difficulty reaching Seatoun. The *Tapuhi* had departed from Queen's Wharf at 7.40 am with her regular crew under Captain Olsen, plus additional crew and pilot Sword. With visibility at times zero the *Tapuhi* made for the relative shelter of Seatoun.

As the *Tapuhi* rounded Kau Point she encountered the full fury of the storm. The wind was at times in excess of 100 knots, so strong that it blew the tug out of control on three occasions, turning her completely around. When the *Tapuhi* was clear of Point Gordon she was guided by radio from the *Tiakina*. As the tug was not fitted with radar, her crew were almost blind. She was guided towards the outer leading light, one of two used to guide shipping into the port. When the *Tapuhi* was halfway there it became obvious she could do nothing at that time to help the *Wahine*. So the *Tiakina* went out to guide her into Worser Bay where they anchored, waiting for conditions to improve. At 9.45 am the *Tiakina* went into Seatoun Wharf to change watches as her crew had been on duty since 11.00 pm the previous night. Only Galloway and Brown remained aboard as the launch returned to anchor with a fresh crew. On board now were engineer Jack Rawlinson and boatmen Ian Feetham and Lockie McLean.

At 10.45 am, with improved visibility, the two vessels proceeded towards Steeple Rock Beacon where they saw the *Wahine* for the first time. The ferry had continued her drift into the harbour and was now only 200 metres south of Steeple Rock. On board the *Tapuhi* a towline was prepared.

Conditions were still too dangerous for the smaller *Tiakina* to try and get alongside the *Wahine*. While the *Tapuhi* was manoeuvred in preparation for an attempt to get a line on board, Galloway asked Captain Brown to steam around the *Wahine* to look for any obvious damage. As they went around the ship they could see both anchor cables extending to the south and the ship rolling rather sluggishly. They saw that the *Wahine* had settled by the stern and that the sill by the stern door was now submerged. This was normally about eight feet above water and indicated that the ferry had considerable hull damage. The ship's lifeboat ladders were now hanging down each side and people in orange lifejackets were on some of the outside decks. For those on board, the sight of the *Tiakina* and *Tapuhi* must have lifted their spirits with the knowledge they were not alone.

After her circuit the pilot launch stood off while the tug made for the *Wahine*. Noting that the ferry was sheering about, Captain Sword managed, with great difficulty, to manoeuvre to within 8 metres of the *Wahine*'s stern, from where a line was fired across to the *Tapuhi*. A tow wire was attached and hauled back to the ferry, and then made fast. As there was no power to the winches the wire was hauled by hand with both vessels moving about quite violently. The hauling of the wire was described in the Court of Inquiry Report as an 'Homeric task, deserving to be noted with admiration for all that joined in.'

Once the wire was secure on the *Wahine* an attempt was made to shorten the anchor cables, so the stricken vessel could be towed more easily. Before this could be accomplished, however, an exceptionally large wave picked up the *Tapuhi* and drew her away from the *Wahine*, snapping the four inch wire like a piece of cotton. Immediately the tug's crew made preparations for another attempt. But the tug was moving around so violently that they once again had to withdraw to the calmer waters off Seatoun. The *Tapuhi*, a former war surplus vessel built in 1945 and designed as a harbour tug, was not designed for salvage work and was underpowered, particularly for this task.

After the towline parted, Captain Galloway noticed that the *Wahine* had swung enough to create some shelter from the oncoming wind and waves. Seizing this opportunity he asked Captain Brown to try and get the *Tiakina* alongside so he could board the ferry, and then alerted the *Wahine*.

With a heavy swell and galeforce winds Captain Brown made his way towards the ferry, aiming for the No. 3 lifeboat ladder on the starboard side. As he approached, the *Tiakina* was being lifted 6-10 metres by the heavy swell. Out on deck Captain Galloway, with one of the launch's crew in attendance, prepared himself to leap from the pilot launch and grab the ladder. In the wheelhouse Captain Brown's main concern was that the launch did not crush Galloway or that he lose his grip and fall into the sea. At 11.55 am when the *Tiakina* was

The Wahine *with liferafts hanging, starboard side. The weather conditions were very bleak while the tug* Tapuhi *stood by, unable to safely manoeuvre to the other side of the* Wahine, *due to the many people in the water.* Evening Post

within range, Galloway leaped, getting a good grip on the ladder and starting his ascent towards the boat deck some 10.5 metres above him. After making good progress, he suddenly slipped down the ladder a couple of rungs. The watching Captain Robertson thought he would surely be crushed against the ship's side by *Tiakina*, as the launch rose and fell on the waves. However, Galloway recovered and continued climbing, while Captain Brown put the *Tiakina's* engines to full astern to back away from the *Wahine*.

At about 12.16 pm the Harbour Master, Captain Suckling, received a message informing him that Captain Galloway had boarded the *Wahine* from the pilot launch *Tiakina*. Captain Galloway's actions under the circumstances must have taken great courage, as was later noted at the Court of Inquiry. The Deputy Harbour Master noted on his way to the bridge that the ship had a list to starboard of about five degrees. Arriving on the bridge he offered his assistance to Captain Robertson.

A courageous man – Captain Galloway – a hero on 10 April 1968, photographed in August 1983. V H Young & L A Sawyer

An Increasing List

With Galloway on board, Captain Robertson now felt he could leave the bridge. At 12.30 pm he and Chief Officer Luly made an inspection of the ship. They started with the stern door on the vehicle deck, which they found to be watertight. However, water was still finding its way onto that deck via parts of the ventilation system. The ship's engineers, led by Chief Engineer Herbert Wareing, attempted to block the ventilators. The engineers were working in difficult conditions with few of the right tools, as flooding in the engine room had made them inaccessible.

Luly noted that there was more water lying on the deck since his earlier inspection. It now covered the vehicle deck from the stern door for about a third of the length of the deck with a depth between five and 38 cm. From the stern door Robertson and Luly continued along the vehicle deck until they reached the stairs leading to F Deck. Peering down they could see that the deck was now flooded.

Within half an hour of boarding the *Wahine*, Galloway noticed the list had increased. It was now between 5 and 22 degrees; though it was impossible to accurately assess the angle because of the ship's movement. When Galloway had first boarded, he felt the *Wahine* was in no immediate danger, but the situation was changing rapidly. He now assessed the list at 25 degrees and increasing.

Still sitting in the smoke room, Shirley Hick noticed that the *Wahine* had developed a slight list to starboard. This had increased perceptibly in about 30 minutes, and many people were beginning to be concerned about their situation. Some of the passengers used the curtains hanging down each window as an inclinometer to gauge

Wahine *Chief Engineer Herbert Wareing. The chief engineer and engine room crew endeavoured to stop water flowing to the main vehicle deck. However, efforts to drain excess water off the deck and down to the engine room presented an impossible challenge, especially as the engineers had only limited tools.* Museum of Wellington City & Sea

the increasing angle. The ship was now rolling more to starboard than to port, and people were becoming anxious and agitated. By 1.00 pm the deck was steep enough for some chairs to topple over and tables to start sliding.

The low barometric pressure made the tide much higher than usual and the extreme wind and sea conditions had forced extra water into the harbour. When the wind started to ease just after 1.00 pm and the tide turned, this extra water started to exit the harbour. At about 1.20 pm the *Wahine*, riding to her anchors with her bow pointing into wind and sea, started to swing with her port side, now facing the weather due to the retreating water. This had the effect of creating a lee or shelter from the worst of the weather. However, it also caused the list of the stricken vessel to increase as the water on the vehicle deck, which had previously been covering much of the open vehicle deck, started to settle more on the starboard side. This made the vessel even more unstable and in serious danger of capsizing.

The ferry's situation was worsening by the minute. The positive feeling of stability was gone, as each time the ship rose and fell to an approaching sea she was now wallowing in the water. Just after 1.00 pm she gave a couple of lurches to starboard, frightening most on board.

Captain Sword on the *Tapuhi* was standing off on the port quarter of the *Wahine* as she made the swing, getting ready to attempt to put another wire rope aboard the ferry. The weather had started to moderate but the wind was still gale force at about 40 knots and with a big sea still running. On the bridge of the *Wahine* Captain

Robertson had positioned himself on the port wing and Captain Galloway was on the starboard wing. When Galloway saw the lee developing he informed Robertson. After conferring, the latter gave the order that every captain dreads - abandon ship. At 1.25 pm Beacon Hill Signal Station received a message from the *Wahine* stating 'all passengers being put in lifeboats, have all trawlers and small craft available sent.'

When Captain Robertson gave the order to abandon ship the chief engineer was on the bridge. Concerned about his men's safety, he rang the engine room and told them to come up on deck. As they emerged from the engine room, he checked them off. One was missing: Third Engineer Theo King. King was eventually located by the second electrician, Roy Langbein, in the forward end of the engine room.

The *Tapuhi* was advised to abandon any attempt to put a wire aboard the ferry and instead prepare to pick up survivors. Vessels of all types started to make their way towards the foundering *Wahine*. The largest to go was the rail ferry *Aramoana*; other smaller coasters, fishing vessels, a navy launch and a variety of pleasure craft battled their way out as fast as they could in the conditions.

Seamen on the poop deck (stern) with the broken tow wire at their feet. The task of hauling the wire on board from the tug Tapuhi *had been an extremely difficult task as the storm raged. The deck seats' disarray is believed to have been caused by a colossal wave that swept over this deck.* David Hendy

The starboard side boat deck. These boats, number one to four (Lifeboat-1 in the foreground) were the only lifeboats to be launched on 10 April 1968 due to the heavy list. Museum of Wellington City & Sea

Right: November 1966 - the Wahine crew practice a weekly lifeboat drill in Lyttelton. Only 15 months later, these boats would be used in a real emergency. Brian Smith

Abandon Ship

Panic surged through the smoke room, and through the other areas where passengers were gathered. Moments after the lurch, alarm bells sounded throughout the ship. The abandon ship order was given and passengers ordered to make their way to the right or starboard side. In the commotion that followed many were separated from loved ones. Earlier, passengers who had felt quite safe had taken off their lifejackets. Now they frantically began looking for them and struggled to get them on. When the ship had lurched, a number of individuals were trapped by the toppling furniture and other loose objects. The crew and some of the passengers helped free these people and get them on their feet.

In the noise and confusion some passengers did not hear the announcements directing them to the starboard side and many made their way to the higher port side. Once there, most found it a daunting task to make their way down the sharply angled deck towards the starboard side. Some passengers tried to get there by retracing their steps through the accommodation; others made their way to the after ends of B and C Decks to get to the lifeboats. In their panic some ran down the tilting deck, only to

lose their footing and go hurtling into the ship's rails or other deck fittings, which caused some serious injuries.

When the Wahine lurched at around 1.00 pm, crockery and other loose objects started crashing to the deck in the cafeteria. David Hendy realised that the situation was changing rapidly for the worse. Some of the men in the cafeteria were asked to help launch the liferafts so David joined the group. As they were about to launch a raft over the side it started to inflate, with the wind catching it and entangling the raft on some of the ship's fittings.

Making his way back to the cafeteria David noticed a group of people moving with difficulty towards a lower deck on the starboard side which was almost in the water. When he finally made it down to the starboard side he paused to take a photograph and looking over the ship's rail, noticed a capsized liferaft. Seizing the moment he climbed over the rail and jumped into the raft. As he landed in the raft, his bulky lifejacket knocked the wind out of him and he just lay there looking skyward trying to catch his breath. As each sea surged past him the liferaft, which was not fully inflated, buckled uneasily.

The raft drifted away from the Wahine and after some time David was rescued by the Tapuhi. Amazingly David still had his camera and once on board the tug he could see other rafts drifting around. While taking another photograph he heard a voice bellow from behind him, "Forget your bloody photographs and come and help your

Alma Hick (three years old) sits with other passengers in the Wahine *smoke room. Alma later tragically lost her life on board lifeboat S1 when it was overwhelmed by huge waves off the Pencarrow Coast.* F. T. Robinson

mates!" It was the captain shouting from up in the wheelhouse. Those words hit him hard and it was not long before he put the camera down and began assisting people on board. A makeshift ladder was put together and hung over the side of the vessel.

With the tug so high out of the water, and rising and falling as each wave passed under, it was extremely difficult to get people on board. Another danger to those in the water was the tug's thrashing propeller which periodically came out of the water as the ship was being tossed about by the rough sea.

Once on board, survivors were taken below into the crew accommodation where they sat crammed like sardines. The space in which David Hendy found himself had the tug's rusty anchor cables running through it down to the cable locker. He remembers sitting crosslegged on the deck next to an elderly man who was sobbing uncontrollably. David put his arm around the man to comfort him, trying to make light of the experience and saying that they were all safe now. A woman sitting opposite quietly informed him that the man had just lost his wife. For several minutes nothing was said, then the woman spoke again, asking if anyone would say the Lord's prayer. David, a Catholic, offered, and led the group in prayer.

Back on the Wahine crew members called out, telling passengers to sit and slide down the deck where other crew would try to catch them. Among the passengers to go to the wrong side were Shirley Hick and her three children. Once outside, Shirley was not sure what to do. The steep deck made her worry for the children. If one of them lost their balance she felt they would have been seriously injured or killed. While she was wondering how to get them all to the starboard side, a male passenger told her that the ship was being abandoned from the other side. She told him that she needed help and he took Alma, saying he would put her into one of the lifeboats. Alma did not want to

Just before David Hendy abandoned ship he took this unbelievable photograph of passengers scrambling to get into liferafts as the Wahine *listed heavy to starboard and the sea began to lap the deck.* David Hendy

A seaman cautiously descends a ladder exposed to the rough weather conditions. It was extremely dangerous to walk about and many accidents occurred onboard; a number of these resulted in severely broken bones. F.T. Robinson

leave her mother and started to cry, refusing to go. Shirley felt she had no choice and spoke sharply to her. To this day Shirley regrets having to do that, but without help the chances of the entire family reaching the starboard side would have been slim. This was the last time she saw Alma alive.

Six year old David, terrified by the steep angle of the deck, would not move. Shirley was now frantic. Just then two stewards appeared. One picked David up and took him down to C Deck. Now only Shirley and Gordon had to get to the rail. The second steward, Bryan McMaster, took Gordon so Shirley could move more easily. All three reached the starboard railing, where the ship's list was now so steep that sea water was lapping the deck. The Chief Officer placed a white Salvus lifejacket around Gordon. It was too big for the baby, but better than nothing. The second steward was now in the water and Gordon was passed to him. Gordon was crying and McMaster tried to comfort him. McMaster placed the baby on his chest and kicked away from the side of the *Wahine*, floating on his back. To make things more difficult, McMaster could not swim a stroke and was totally reliant on his lifejacket.

Shirley now left the ship. She was unable to see McMaster or Gordon but could hear the baby crying, which upset her. As she lowered herself into the cold water she thought of the other children, wondering where they were and if they were all right. As she drifted away from the *Wahine* she could still hear Gordon, but after a while he stopped crying. She feared he had drowned. Drifting about all she could hear was the sound of the waves around her. Despairing and in a state of shock she became convinced that all the children must be dead and blamed herself for their deaths.

Each time she was on top of the swell, she could see the Picton ferry *Aramoana* and this gave her hope and something to focus on. The *Aramoana* had lowered both

its motorised lifeboats with volunteer crews, one under the Chief Officer Charles Graham and the other under Second Officer John King. Shirley Hick was the first person to be rescued by John King and his crew.

She had been in the water for about an hour and had drifted towards the Pencarrow coast. Seeing the high sided lifeboat coming over the large swell and bearing down on her worried her for a moment. With some difficulty the boat crew hauled her aboard. They made her comfortable and asked if she had been alone. Then one of the crew noticed another survivor in the water and the lifeboat headed towards him. Getting the elderly man aboard was difficult but the crew were determined.

Just as they were tending to the man a huge wave picked up the lifeboat and flipped it end over end, spilling its occupants into the sea. Two of the boat's crew struggled ashore through the rocks on the eastern shore. King had a firm grip on Shirley and both were clinging to the upturned boat with two others from the crew - the elderly man was adrift nearby.

Fortunately, the trawler *Seaway* was also out looking for survivors and came across the lifeboat not long after the capsize. A lifeline with a lifebuoy attached was thrown to those holding on to the lifeboat and one by one they were hauled aboard, Shirley first. They also managed to get the elderly man aboard. The crew of the *Seaway* made them all comfortable and continued to look for survivors. Not finding any more, they made their way back to the Inter-Island Wharf, opposite the Wellington Railway Station, where the *Wahine* should have berthed that morning.

As they steamed back into the harbour the sea was now calm. Once away from the disaster area it was hard to believe what had happened earlier. It was like waking from a nightmare.

At the wharf Shirley and the others were taken to the railway station, which had been set up to process survivors and give medical assistance. Shirley was stripped of her wet clothes and a deep cut on her leg was given attention. By this time she was deeply chilled and in an effort to restore her circulation, given a massage. When the helpers realised she was pregnant Shirley was told an ambulance would take her to hospital. She asked about her children but at that time no one could help her. She was in utter despair.

A policeman assisted Shirley towards the ambulance, fending off all the media who had gathered to report on the disaster. As survivors staggered off the buses which had carried them to railway station, the look of relief and shock on their faces was still very apparent. Police, Red Cross workers, medical staff and other volunteers greeted survivors and tried to comfort and care for them. As Shirley got to the ambulance some one informed her that a small baby was in intensive care at Wellington Hospital. Her spirits were raised and then she was told that David was in Hutt Hospital. She suddenly felt much better – but there was still no news of Alma.

Time to abandon ship as the Wahine *rolls heavily to the lower side. There were major concerns that the ferry would roll over before passengers were able to evacuate. The dark objects in the water are lifeboats (left) and life-rafts (right). Due to the horrendous wind conditions several empty liferafts were blown away from the ship. Various young and fit passengers preferred to jump into the sea rather than risk the lifeboats or liferafts.* Evening Post

The Wahine *seriously lists off Steeple Rock while rescue vessels and the rail ferry* Aramoana *gather round to assist with the rescue of people leaving the ferry.* Evening Post

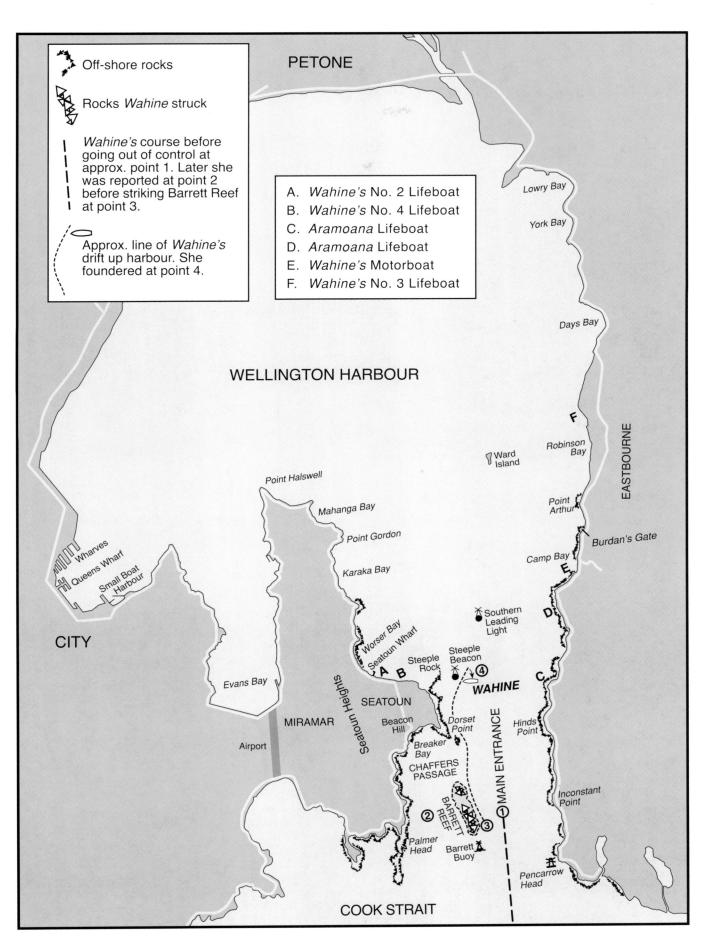

PETONE

Off-shore rocks

Rocks *Wahine* struck

Wahine's course before going out of control at approx. point 1. Later she was reported at point 2 before striking Barrett Reef at point 3.

Approx. line of *Wahine's* drift up harbour. She foundered at point 4.

A. *Wahine's* No. 2 Lifeboat
B. *Wahine's* No. 4 Lifeboat
C. *Aramoana* Lifeboat
D. *Aramoana* Lifeboat
E. *Wahine's* Motorboat
F. *Wahine's* No. 3 Lifeboat

Lowry Bay
York Bay
Days Bay

WELLINGTON HARBOUR

Robinson Bay

EASTBOURNE

Ward Island

Point Halswell

Mahanga Bay

Point Arthur

Burdan's Gate

Point Gordon

Camp Bay

Karaka Bay

Wharves
Queens Wharf
Small Boat Harbour

Southern Leading Light

CITY

Worser Bay
Seatoun Wharf

Steeple Rock

Steeple Beacon

④

WAHINE

Evans Bay

Hinds Point

SEATOUN

MIRAMAR

Seatoun Heights

Beacon Hill

Dorset Point

Airport

Breaker Bay
CHAFFERS PASSAGE

① MAIN ENTRANCE

Inconstant Point

②

BARRETT REEF

③

Palmer Head

Barrett Buoy

Pencarrow Head

COOK STRAIT

Map showing where the lifeboats landed and the track of the ship through the harbour entrance.

The Hick Family Story

The steward McMaster and baby Gordon had suffered from seasickness due to the motion of the swells still sweeping into the harbour. About 30 minutes after they left the *Wahine*, a large wave swept Gordon away from McMaster. Unable to see the baby, the steward did his best to find him. Shortly after the sound of an outboard motor gave hope of rescue as a privately owned runabout owned by Jim Toulis appeared over the top of the swell. Seeing McMaster in the water, Jim's crewman Bill Bell was able to drag him aboard. McMaster's heart sank when he saw the little figure of Gordon in the bottom of the boat. Bell had picked up the baby only minutes before.

Jim had found out about the *Wahine*'s plight when a friend called him at the Terminus Milk Bar which the Toulis family owned on Lambton Quay. As he lived in Seatoun, Jim decided to go and see what was happening. When he finally arrived at Seatoun he found a number of people gathered on the beach watching. Seeing the ferry's heavy list, he decided to get his crew together and see if they could do anything to help.

Toulis and his crew, who launched their boat at Worser Bay, became the first privately owned rescue craft on the scene. A seasoned boat handler used to the rough conditions so quickly whipped up on the shores of Cook Strait, Toulis steered his small boat around groups of survivors looking for those who needed immediate rescue.

People in the water directed them to three elderly women and two elderly men who were in a bad way. With all these people onboard, the 5 metre boat, which was in the main shipping channel and exposed to enormous waves, became sluggish and almost capsized. One wave picked it up and dropped it hard on the next wave. Toulis heard a loud crack and soon realised that a number of the boat's ribs had broken. A blanket had also been tangled around the propeller, which Bill Bell cleared. Toulis also recalls seeing handbags and other items drifting about. He decided it would be prudent to head in to Seatoun and land the survivors for treatment.

While making their way slowly to Seatoun beach, they passed many people in the water. Toulis and his crewman could only focus on their own situation and hope that others would come out to help those still in the water. Once ashore the rescued survivors received medical care and were made comfortable before being taken to the Wellington Railway Station. Little Gordon Hick also received medical attention and attempts were made to

Jim Toulis and crew aboard his five metre runabout were the first to reach Wahine *survivors in the water, saving many from certain death. Toulis' extensive knowledge and experience of Wellington's south coast proved invaluable throughout the rescue operations.* J Toulis

Right: Survivors and rescue workers at Seatoun Beach. A fellow survivor comforts Clarence O'Neill (seven years old), who came ashore in Lifeboat-S4, along with his parents and five other siblings. Evening Post

revive him. After strenuous efforts a flicker of life returned. He was rushed to Wellington Hospital and placed in intensive care.

Jim Toulis and Bill Bell, now joined by Jim's brother-in-law Colin Athea, headed out again. This time they towed one of the lifeboats in towards Seatoun beach. As they got closer in, a larger vessel took over the tow and Jim turned the boat towards Pencarrow. But it was too rough for the open boat and they returned to Seatoun.

When Alma and her temporary guardian finally made their way to the starboard lifeboat deck, she had been put into the motorised lifeboat, one of four on that side. Not as big as the other three, this lifeboat was designed to carry fifty people. In charge of the boat was Third Officer Grahame Noblett. Once loaded, it was lowered to the water and managed to get away from the ship's side without too much trouble.

When clear of the *Wahine* , Noblett manuoevred the boat to pick up people already in the water. With a full complement aboard, the lifeboat soon became overloaded. People were lying on top of each other and some passengers underneath struggled to get enough air. Water started to enter the boat. This could have been coming from one of the plugs in the bottom, which had been accidentally knocked out. Soon the water was high enough to stop the engine. With the boat's built-in buoyancy tanks, it could not sink. However, it settled down to sea level and many onboard were washed out or jumped. The tug *Tapuhi* was nearby, but suddenly the lifeboat was picked up by a large wave and capsized,

trapping some of its passengers. One of those trapped was Alma Hick.

The luckiest of Shirley Hick's children was David. Drifting towards Eastbourne aboard a flotation seat he tried to assist an elderly man who was in the water onto the raft. Unable to do so, the man lost his grip and drifted away. David Hick was fortunate. Somehow he managed to get to Eastbourne. Stripped of all clothing by the sea, he was taken to Hutt Hospital for treatment.

When Shirley arrived at Wellington Hospital, she found that the baby in intensive care was indeed Gordon. However, his ordeal was not over. He had serious brain damage because of the time taken to revive him. Shirley, distraught at this news, was admitted to hospital. There was still no word of Alma. Meanwhile a tally of the deaths was being compiled and publicised. Shirley began to give up hope for her little girl. The following day she received the heartbreaking news that Alma's body had been found on the Pencarrow coast.

In the Water

The Wahine *rolls and settles to the seabed while the rail-ferry* Aramoana *stands by. Though the* Aramoana *crew valiantly attempted to save people, the ferry's high sides made it impossible for survivors to swim in and climb up. The* Aramoana *thus launched two motor-powered lifeboats crewed by volunteers to pick up survivors. Unfortunately, one lifeboat capsized while the other was swept onto the Pencarrow coast.*
Evening Post

Before the order to abandon ship, when it became obvious that the portside lifeboats could not be launched due to the heavy list, seamen, among them deck boy Alan Windsor, were ordered to launch the liferafts on the higher port side. They rolled the liferaft cannisters down the ship's steeply angled side and then pulled on the painter (this rope attached the liferafts to the ship). By pulling on the rope, the gas cylinder within, inflated the liferafts. Unfortunately as soon as the rafts inflated they were caught by the wind and went flying in the air like kites, still tethered to the ship. Realising the futility of their efforts, the seamen focused on the liferafts on the starboard side.

Though the lifeboats and liferafts on the port side of the *Wahine* could not be launched, ample life saving equipment was carried to save all those on board. The 30 liferafts alone had a capacity of 750 people. However, the heavy list also made it very difficult for those on board to move about safely. Once passengers reached the lifeboats they had to jump a gap of about a metre to get on board. For many elderly people this was a terrifying experience and some had to be forcibly put into the boats. The vessel was rolling heavily, making the evacuation more dangerous. Many people preferred to take their chances by jumping into the sea rather than risk getting in the boats. It was with great difficulty that the crew managed to finally get all the passengers off the sinking ship.

Looking back, Alan still feels proud of the way everyone worked together to get passengers and crew off the ship. After working with the other seamen to evacuate the vessel, Alan left with the bosun, George Hampson. With the water lapping the deck, the two men stepped into the sea where nearby an empty liferaft floated. On reaching it they had great difficulty climbing in. Alan, dragged down by his coat and work boots, stripped them off. By now the bosun had managed to get into the raft and helped him onboard. They then cut the painter and the raft started drifting away from the ship. The raft drifted up the harbour, lifted by each passing swell. Each time it reached the crest of a swell, the two men stared anxiously out the doorway. They also watched the *Wahine* start to slowly roll onto her starboard side.

The sound of cargo, furniture and equipment crashing within the ship surprised them. Alan had been afraid of being trapped onboard when the ship rolled over. Seeing this happening after he had left the ship made him feel glad to be in the liferaft and grateful to be alive.

The two seamen were not adrift very long before being rescued by the *Tiakina* which towed them back to Seatoun Wharf. From there they were put on a bus with other survivors and taken to the Railway Station where they were given hot soup and blankets. Alan then went home to Titahi Bay, just north of Wellington, only to find that his parents had gone into the city to look for him.

Shortly before the *Wahine* rolled over, the last two people left on board jumped into the sea. First Captain Galloway and then, after a final look around, Captain

Soon after foundering, the Wahine *rolled and slowly settled to the harbour seabed. Aboard the* Tuna*, a small pilot boat working as a rescue craft, were Harbour Board divers Morunga and Oliver. When the* Wahine *appeared settled, they swam over and managed to get onboard. However, as they searched for survivors they could still feel the wreck moving. Oliver recalls: "it was as if the ship was crying." Hearing the various creaks, knocks and scraping noises, plus the sight of luggage, clothing, and shoes floating all around was extremely eerie.*
Evening Post

Robertson joined the Deputy Harbour Master in the water. They soon drifted clear of the stricken ship.

After about 30 minutes the second privately owned launch on the scene came upon Galloway and Robertson. Owned by Joe Bown, the *Cuda* had earlier picked up four survivors. Getting these two into the *Cuda* was extremely difficult. Both were big men, and their wet woollen uniforms made the task almost impossible.

Once on board, Captain Robertson asked the launch's owner if he would take it close to the *Wahine* so he could satisfy himself that no one was still on board. Just then the ship rolled onto her starboard side. Robertson watched as water poured into the ship's funnel and a great puff of steam escaped from the boilers. As the launch headed towards Seatoun Wharf he was silent.

Rescuers and others ashore looked on in horror as the once proud vessel rolled. Not far away, the rail ferry *Aramoana* stood by helplessly as the *Wahine* settled onto the seabed.

The first of the ship's boats to reach safety was lifeboat S2 under command of fourth engineer Philip Bennett. The boat was towed to Seatoun beach where it was followed by lifeboat S4. During the morning, emergency personnel had gathered on the beach, waiting to see if their services would be required. Due to the serious damage occurring elsewhere around Wellington, the storm put a heavy strain on resources.

When the *Cuda* arrived at the wharf, Robertson was met by the Union Company's Chief Marine

Superintendent, Captain Arthur Crosbie. The shaken captain was put in a company car and taken home. He is quoted as saying 'When I walked through the doorway I had no feeling at all. I just felt numb.' Mrs Robertson tried to comfort and help him out of his uniform, but he just stood there, in shock. Eventually she managed to get him into dry clothes, though he would neither eat nor take a hot bath.

Below: *Lifeboat-S2 arriving at Seatoun Wharf – Fourth Engineer Philip Bennett (standing up in the lifeboat on left) heroically rescued numerous survivors from the sea.* Dominion and Sunday Times

Wahine *Lifeboat S4 (starboard), Seatoun Beach. Rescue workers hasten to take hold of the painter, endeavouring to haul the lifeboat into the shallows. People ashore presumed this beach would be the main landing for many more survivors with the arrival of Lifeboat S2 and Lifeboat-S4, but unfortunately this was not to be. Lifeboat S4 was under command of Quarter Master Tom Dartford.* Evening Post

Wahine *Able Seaman George Brabander, Seatoun Beach - carries a young child from Lifeboat S4. Earlier, he had jumped into the stormy sea and saved a baby by floating along on his back. The baby lay on his lifejacket until it was safely placed aboard the lifeboat. In addition, Brabander untangled a rope that had become twisted around the lifeboat propeller and rudder, an extreme effort under the rough sea conditions.* Evening Post

Chief officer Rodney Luly coming ashore at Seatoun Beach. Miss Europa, a Worser Bay Surf Club boat, had managed to pick up Luly and another crew member. Later, the salvage company that removed the wreck of the Wahine, *employed Luly in a professional capacity.*   Evening Post

An Eastwards Drift

After the vessel was finally abandoned, those waiting onshore at Seatoun were caught by surprise when they realised that those in the water and others in liferafts and lifeboats were in fact being carried across the harbour entrance to the rocky shore of Pencarrow. The drift to the further shore was caused by the now outgoing tide and the still very bad weather conditions. This unforeseen development was to cost many people their lives. Rescue authorities frantically made arrangements to get personnel around to the eastern shore but with all the chaos the storm had caused ashore, it took time to reach survivors on that side of the harbour.

Rescue craft did their best to save people in the water before they reached the dangerous rocks. But once the boats, rafts and people in the water were swept into shallow water, rescue craft had to stand off for their own safety. They could only watch helplessly as people disappeared into the surf only to be dashed onto the rocks and seriously injured or killed.

As police, army, medical personnel and other rescuers arrived they were confronted with horrific sights. Bodies were scattered around on the beach. Survivors tried to make their way to Eastbourne, the nearest suburb on the Pencarrow coast. Many had broken bones or had been stripped of clothing as they were swept through the surf and were staggering about, disorientated due to shock and hypothermia. In some cases they clambered up the beach thinking they had made it ashore. But before anyone could reach them, a large wave would wash up the beach and sweep them back out to sea where they drowned.

Seatoun Wharf - Rescue workers carry weary survivors, unable to walk, as ambulances stand-by to take them to Wellington Public Hospital. Evening Post

Below: Survivors land at Seatoun Wharf in a Zodiac (one of the smallest rescue craft owned by the Civil Aviation Department Fire Brigade from Wellington Airport). In the late 1960s these craft were deployed to pick up aeroplane crash survivors. However, with their simple manoeuvrability and great speed, they made perfect ship-rescue vessels. Evening Post

Rescuers and Survivors

Eastbourne – rescue workers stand by to assist possible survivors inside a liferaft being swept through the surf. Unlike lifeboats, liferafts just have paddles to move them through the water. These liferafts were designed to move away from the side of the ship, and once clear, to drift about until a motorised vessel fastened them in tow. Any survivors in the liferafts were at the mercy of the elements due to the harrowing wind and sea conditions. I. McFarlane

Rescue workers seize the liferaft before it is swept out to sea. I. McFarlane

Detective Ray Whitham

Two of the police officers ordered to head for the Pencarrow coast were detectives Ray Whitham and Rangi Rangihaka. The morning had started badly for Ray as he had attended a house fire in Newtown where an elderly woman living on her own died as a result of an overturned kerosene heater. Driving to Petone from Wellington meant travelling along the Hutt Road on the harbour foreshore. The road was covered in rubble and the breaking waves came right across the railway line on the seaward side of the road. It was still raining heavily and with the sea spray they could only see about 50 metres. Debris off buildings was scattered everywhere.

Over the police radio they heard that one person was confirmed dead from the *Wahine*. This made the two men realise the seriousness of that vessel's situation. Ray Whitham remembers peering out the car window towards the harbour and thinking that there could be a terrible death toll. They had no real idea where the ferry was and what was happening aboard.

When they finally got to Eastbourne and Burdon's Gate they were met by Lower Hutt Senior Sergeant Brian Courtney and a group of police constables. His instructions were to head south along the shoreline and do whatever they could. Three other police officers joined Ray and Rangi as they set off along the dirt road which

Left: Shocked and exhausted, survivors rest on the back of a four-wheel-drive which cautiously manoeuvres along the beach towards Burdon's Gate. Evening Post

Lower left: Near Burdon's Gate, Eastbourne – rescue workers prepare an ambulance for survivors. Evening Post

Below: Police constables and cadets from the Trentham Training College assist a shocked survivor. The rescue workers witnessed many horrific scenes along the coast. I. McFarlane

wound its way to the Pencarrow lighthouse. None of them knew what to expect.

As they trudged along the road, Ray remembers two college boys, Bruce Mitchell and John Sarginson, both about 17 years old, asking if they could join them. Ray agreed but told them to stick with the group.

The coastline is predominantly rocky on the east coast of the harbour, though interspersed with small gravel beaches. The dirt road was impassable for vehicles as it was covered with slips, rubble, kelp and driftwood, with parts of it deeply scoured by the surging seas. As they struggled along Ray began to wonder if they had been sent on a fool's errand. They had been looking for some time and had found no one. But on rounding the next point they came across their first group of survivors. Almost all were barefoot, painfully picking their way through the rubble and sharp stones. They were bedraggled, cold and wet with most in various states of semi-undress. Many were bleeding, some were crying, and all looked very shaken.

Some asked for help, others were disorientated and didn't know where they were. Some just stared blindly ahead and walked on. The rescue group could not even offer them a blanket as they themselves only had what

they stood in. All they could do was reassure the survivors and tell them to keep walking as help was not far away.

As the policemen and the young college boys pressed on along the coast, they started to fully realise the extent of the disaster and to appreciate that time was of the essence. The waves were still crashing into the shore. Ray estimates they were 6 to 9 metres high. He had grown up on the North Island's west coast and played on surf beaches but these were bigger than anything he had seen before. The noise from the surf was very loud and the men often had to shout to each other.

Further around the coast in Camp Bay, the rescuers came across an upturned lifeboat. It was the motor boat from the *Wahine*. As they got closer they saw a man with his leg trapped underneath. He was surging in and out as each wave swept past him. The men rushed over, only to find he was dead. John Sarginson was then sent back to Burdon's Gate to inform the police what they had found and to stress that medical supplies, blankets and stretchers would be urgently required.

They tried to lift the boat to free the man's body but found it far too heavy. The sight of the first casualty was upsetting and they believed that things were going to get a lot worse. They passed more survivors, which by now

An elderly couple can still manage a smile after their ordeal as they head for Burdon's Gate. Dominion, Sunday Times.

had become a steady stream of people. Their spirits were lifted when they came across a small group of police officers they knew who had been returning from Christchurch after giving evidence at a court case. These men were young and fit, and trained to have good survival instincts. One of them told Ray that conditions were so bad that he didn't think he was going to make it.

As they reached another bay, they saw survivors lying exhausted on the beach at the waterline. Others were trying to crawl up the beach with water surging around them. Some were still in the water desperately trying to reach safety. In an effort to help these people Ray and the others rushed into the water, sometimes up to their chests, to grab survivors and drag them onto the shore. On a couple of occasions Ray had to brace himself against the rocks to keep from being dragged out to sea by the receding waves.

While trying to rescue a young male survivor who had washed in totally exhausted, Ray tried to reach his outstretched hand but the young man was carried out by the receding sea. All Ray could do was watch helplessly as he was washed back in on the next wave which then dumped him on the rocks. Ray and one of the others eventually reached him and carried his lifeless body up the beach. He was bloodied all over from deep lacerations and his clothes and lifejacket were badly shredded. Not

able to find a pulse, they presumed he was dead and moved along the beach.

After dragging survivors from the surf, the rescuers pulled them up the beach away from the waterline. They made them as comfortable as possible, propping them up against driftwood or shrubs.

While both men and women, young and old were washed up, Ray remembers that often the elderly women were the most distressed. Ray tried to comfort one elderly woman who was very frightened, cold and tearful. He sat with her a while trying to calm her before returning to the water for others, and finally had to prise his hand from her tight grip. He returned a little later to find she had died.

Mostly the rescuers dragged people out of the surf and off the rocks. The survivors were very cold and it was difficult at a glance to determine if they were alive or dead. So many needed urgent medical attention but this group of six could do nothing more than save them from the water.

Visibility was still very poor. When looking out to sea, the rescuers usually couldn't see survivors until they would pop up as they surged through the surf. On one occasion Ray recalls seeing through the sea spray a large liferaft about 50 metres from shore with perhaps six people onboard being picked up by a huge wave and capsized. He could only hope the people onboard would float in safely.

One of the survivors Ray found was a young officer from the *Wahine* who still had his officer's jacket on but had been stripped of his trousers and shoes. He called out as Ray approached him but on reaching him, Ray could see he had been critically injured as he was swept in over the rocks. His lower abdomen was bleeding extensively and he was very pale, cold and shivering. Ray tried to make him comfortable but the young officer smiled and died in his arms. Ray laid him on the beach and walked away feeling numb and helpless.

At this point, Ray noted that the wind had eased considerably, and that a lot more rescuers had made their way around the coast. He and another policeman, Alan Wyeth, decided they should walk around to another bay to make sure that there was nobody else there. By now the light was getting poor and the two men could only just make out a person stranded on rocks about 60 metres away. When they reached Jack Lysaght, he was crouched naked on a rocky ledge, so drained of strength that he could not climb a two metres to safety. The waves were still washing over him and he was in danger of being washed off. The two policemen managed to get to him and drag him up to high ground and safety. He was not actually from the *Wahine* but from the yacht *Tahi Miranda* . This 10 metre boat had gone out to rescue survivors but became a casualty itself when it was swamped by a huge wave near the entrance to the harbour. All four crew members made it to safety near Hinds Point.

Jack had been swept in by the raging surf, only to be swept out again. When the yacht had sunk he smashed his shoulder and was unable to grab the rocks as he was washed into the shore. As the sea once again carried him towards the rocks Jack knew this would be his last chance; if he did not get a hold of something it would be the end. This time he was washed over rocks, badly lacerating his skull and upper back. Wondering what to do as he could not pull himself up the ledge he was thankful the two policemen arrived in time.

Jack Lysaght was a marine engineer and was well used to the mood of the sea, but he had never experienced the weather conditions of 10 April.

Ray gave the man his jacket and they started to make their way back to Eastbourne. As they started back they were met by a four wheel drive vehicle. Front end loaders had opened up the road so four wheel drive vehicles were coming through to pick up survivors and bring more rescue personnel. The others jumped aboard but Ray chose to walk despite the long trek back. He trudged along, numb from the cold and the terrible sights, just wanting to be alone. He passed people and vehicles heading in the opposite direction, thinking they were probably far too late. Physically exhausted and emotionally spent, Ray had nothing more to give; it was up to others to continue the work.

The survivors were taken to the Eastbourne RSA where they were given hot drinks and medical treatment. From there they were taken to hospital or, if still able to walk, to the Wellington Railway Station. Rescue efforts went on through the afternoon and into the night. There were many people both ashore and afloat who put the safety of others before their own lives that day.

Survivors slowly make their way along the foreshore of the Pencarrow Coast. Amazingly, the two women in the foreground are still clutching their handbags, even though they came ashore through the surf. Dominion, Sunday Times

In mountainous seas, 174 people were rescued by the tug Tapuhi. *Today there is a living memorial to the tug* Tapuhi *at Oriental Bay. The floating restaurant 'Tugboat on the Bay' is housed on the former twin-screw steam tug* Aucklander, *which has been renamed* Tapuhi II, *in honour of the noble task* Tapuhi *did on 10 April 1968.*
V.H. Young and L.A. Sawyer

A Long Way from Home

David Hendy

After a valiant effort the *Tapuhi* returned to the Inter-island Wharf with its cargo of survivors. David Hendy was now feeling the effects of his ordeal. He was cold and his spirits were low, but he was alive and glad to have finally made it to shore. As he and others came ashore they were met by a police constable who directed them to the railway station where their names and addresses would be taken. Having done that, David was then given something to eat and a hot cup of tea which helped to re-energize him. He noticed there was a small post office at the railway station. Not wanting his friend in Christchurch or his parents in Wales to worry, he arranged for two telegrams to be sent.

Looking back, David believes he must have looked odd to people as he wandered around the city trying to find accommodation. He was soaking wet with rust marks all over his trousers and coat. He tried several hotels but they were full and he ended up going into a printing office to ask for directions. When the staff found out he had been on the *Wahine,* they welcomed him and took him down to the boiler room where he was able to dry his clothes.

One of the staff suggested that, as he was supposed to be travelling on the *Southern Cross* the following day, he should go directly to the ship. A free taxi ride later he arrived at the ship and was taken aboard, made comfortable and given a long hot bath.

That night sleep came easy but the next day his body was stiff and bruised. Despite not having identification, staff at the Commonwealth Bank arranged all the paperwork and money for his leaving New Zealand. One of the local shops also supplied David with some new clothing. On the afternoon of 11 April 1968, David Hendy departed Wellington for South Africa. As the *Southern Cross* sailed past the *Wahine*, David stood by the rail looking at the ship, grateful to be alive and thinking of those who lost their lives.

Arriving home in the United Kingdom four months later after a short stay in South Africa, his mother explained to him how a telegram arrived which read "Wet but Safe and Well. Love Dave", something which made no sense to her. One hour later reading the Daily Mail, shock headlines read "*NZ Ferry Sinks: Huge Loss of Life*".

Camp Bay, Pencarrow Coast – Wahine *lifeboat S1 lies battered and broken on the beach. Along this coastline, 223 survivors came ashore and 47 lifeless bodies were recovered. Four dead were picked up by rescue craft.* Evening Post

Passengers and crew line the decks of the steamer express-ferry Maori, *sadly observing the wreck of the* Wahine *a day after the disaster.* Evening Post

An Act of God

The storm claimed 51 lives from the passengers and crew of the *Wahine*. Most of the deaths occurred on the Pencarrow coast, and one life was lost ashore. The whole country was in shock. Messages of sympathy came from heads of states around the world. In her message the Queen offered her sympathy to the relatives of those who lost their lives.

The destruction caused by the storm in many parts of New Zealand was bad enough but the fact that a vessel the size of the *Wahine* had sunk on the doorstep of the capital city, in full view of many people and television cameras, was unprecedented in New Zealand. That night when people turned on their television to see the day's events they heard NZBC news presenter Dougal Stephenson announce 'Today Wellington is a stricken city.' Though powerful, these words did not come close to describing the fearful conditions experienced on 10 April 1968. Even though graphic images took the disaster right into people's homes, many still found it hard to believe. Copies of the day's news coverage were sent to overseas networks including CBS, ITN and ABC. The NZBC later won a World Newsfilm Award for this coverage, its first major contribution to international news.

On 25 June 1968 a Court of Inquiry was convened to try and determine what caused the loss of the *Wahine* and 51 lives. After hearing from many who had been involved in the disaster, the Court found that neither the master nor the chief officer were guilty of any wrongful acts or defaults. It did note serious omissions or errors of judgement, occurring under conditions of great difficulty and danger, but ruled that these did not not amount to wrongful acts or defaults as charged. The Court made a number of recommendations to help avert a similar disaster in the future.

> *The Court of Inquiry*
> *Proceedings started on 25 June 1968 and lasted 26 days. After hearing evidence from 81 witnesses, the court ruled that the prime cause of the tragedy was that the ship had encountered the worst storm ever recorded in New Zealand. Therefore, the ship sheered off course in zero visibility, went out of human control, and struck Barrett Reef, sustaining serious underwater damage. The immediate cause of the eventual capsize was determined to be the free surface water on the vehicle deck.*

The Court of Inquiry into the disaster listening to evidence.
Museum of Wellington City & Sea

Right: *Wreckage washed up on shore at Eastbourne Beach. A graphic reminder of 10 April 1968.* Alexander Turnbull Library EP/ 1968/1578-F

Below: *An oil slick drifts about the* Wahine *wreck, approximately 400 metres off Seatoun shore. Once the pride of the Union Steam Ship Company, the state of the art ferry lay abandoned only one day after the tragedy. The lifeboats (port side) still in the davits, were unable to be launched, and two inflatable liferafts are still attached to the wreck.* Evening Post

Captain Hector Gordon Robertson

A seafarer all his life, Captain Hector Gordon Robertson started as a Deck-Boy in 1927. He progressed through the ranks, studied for a Deck Officer qualification and on 17 August 1938 was appointed Third Officer of the Union Steam Ship Company cargo vessel *Waipahi*. Between 1938 and 1943 he served on various coastal and trans-Tasman cargo vessels. On 19 November 1943 he was promoted to Chief Officer, serving on cargo vessels and the passenger ships *Monowai, Wahine* (I), *Hinemoa* and *Rangatira (I)*. Between May 1962 and 1966 Captain Robertson held command on a variety of the Company's cargo vessels and on the Wellington to Picton ferry *Tamahine*. In 1962 he commanded New Zealand's first roll-on-roll-off vessel, the rail ferry *Aramoana*, remaining on that ship until December 1965. He then spent a short period on the *Hinemoa* and *Maori* until he was appointed to the Union Company's flag ship on 31 October 1966, taking over from retiring master Captain E. G. K. Meatyeard.

The Union Company only appointed Senior Masters to the steamer express service. These individuals had to have superior ship handling skills, an ability to communicate well with passengers and be able to manage their crew in an efficient manner. They also had to have the ability to deal with all the unions represented onboard in such a way to avoid industrial problems. Captain Robertson, who possessed all these qualities and abilities, was one of the company's top masters.

Captain H.G. Robertson photographed on the bridge of the Wahine. Alexander Turnbull Library c-21105

Below: *Captain Robertson after being landed at Seatoun by the launch* Cuda*, confers with the Marine Superintendent of the Union Steam Ship Company, Captain Arthur Crosbie, and a police officer.* Dominion, Sunday Times

Salvaging the Wreck

Only two days after the storm the weather was calm enough to allow officials to visit the ship, which lay on her side, only partly submerged. Soon after, plans were made to dispose of the remains. A salvage contract was awarded to the United Salvage Company of Melbourne, Australia. United Salvage proposed to refloat the hulk using polystyrene foam and towing it out to sea where it would have been sunk in the depths of Cook Strait. It was estimated that the work required to prepare and carry out the sinking would take approximately two years.

Twelve months into the project another southerly storm broke the wreck into three sections, making refloating impossible. It was then decided to remove the wreck by cutting it into 30 to 80 ton sections to be carried ashore by the Harbour Board's floating crane *Hikitia*.

Divers and workers inspect the wreck a few days after the disaster. The day after the Wahine *sank a local reported hearing tapping sounds coming from the hull. Six Police divers were rushed out to the wreck. They clambered along the hull to where the sounds had been heard, fearing that survivors might be trapped on board. There was no response from tapping on the hull, however each time a swell passed by there was an eerie creaking. It was assumed this creaking sound was what the local had heard. The divers looked through some of the portholes and windows and saw the lounges filled with floating chairs in oily water. Most of the portholes had loose material and books floating against the glass. All the cabins were a total mess though a few were still dry.* Evening Post

Much of the metal work was sent to scrap mills in Auckland for melting down into steel reinforcing for the building industry. The timber work, plastic panelling, fittings and furniture went to the Wellington rubbish dump.

For most of the salvage period the Holm Shipping Company coastal cargo vessel *Holmpark* was used as a base and moored just off the wreck. During the salvage Mr Clive Collett, a diver, was killed in an underwater explosion and there were two cases of the bends. The six divers engaged in the salvage spent 17,000 diving hours on the project and were responsible for cutting 6,500 tons of steel.

Wellington, May 1969 - the Wahine *, with a large crane attached, is hidden from view by sweeping waves. Eventually the violent sea broke the wreck into three pieces.* Evening Post

Harbour Board and salvage company officials at Seatoun Wharf. From left: Harbour Board Chief Engineer A J H Huthison; Harbour Master Captain William (Bill) Galloway; Captain Fant; United Salvage Proprietory Ltd of Australia Diver Jack Edwards; Deputy Harbour Master Captain Cyril Sword. This team of officials inspected the Wahine *wreck on 30 May 1968.* Museum of Wellington City & Sea

For five years the wreck of the *Wahine* lay near the harbour entrance. The last pieces of the ship were lifted from the harbour in September 1973. Until then, the remains were a constant reminder of the tragic events of 10 April 1968. The pride of the Union Steam Ship Company for less than two years, the once proud ship became a symbol of the power of nature over technology and a tragedy which touched the country and the world.

The salvage ship Holmpark *(employed as a base ship) anchored by the* Wahine *wreck. Poor weather delayed diving on many occasions, and practically 30 per cent of working time was lost. One diver was killed in an underwater explosion during the dangerous and challenging salvage process.* Evening Post

Facing page: *The* Wahine's *60 ton bridge section at Fryatt Quay. This section, covered with rotting marine growth, was removed from the wreck by the floating crane* Hikitia *seven months after the disaster.* Museum of Wellington City & Sea

Vehicles being placed on the side of the Wahine *prior to being brought ashore. During the removal of the wreck the cars on the vehicle decks were removed through a hole cut into the hull. A few were later sold in auction.* Evening Post

Bow sections (name of ship, left section) at Queen's Wharf, Wellington. In parts of the hull, mud and silt had accumulated, which made some of these sections difficult to lift. Having been cut up and transported to Auckland, the section pieces were melted into reinforcing rods. V.H. Young and L.A.Sawyer

Conclusion

The wreck of the *Wahine* was a terrible tragedy and one of New Zealand's worst maritime disasters. That day Wellington's emergency and civilian services were severely put to the test. The fact that the *Wahine* stayed afloat for so long after sustaining such serious damage is largely due to the efforts of her officers and crew. Since the sinking of the *Wahine* there have been two roll on roll off passenger ferries operating in European waters, the *Herald of Free Enterprise* and *Estonia*, which sank with terrible loss of life. Roll-on roll-off vessels are much more vulnerable to capsize because of their large open vehicle spaces. Both of these vessels sank in different circumstances to the *Wahine* and their crews did not have an opportunity to mount an organised abandonment. This could have been the fate of the *Wahine* if the ship had not drifted into the harbour.

For the *Wahine*'s crew to evacuate 733 people in the short time available was amazing given the situation. Unfortunately no one ashore had thought of the problem of survivors being swept to the Pencarrow coast on the outgoing tide. Even if rescuers had been in position it is probable that people would have still died coming through the surf, given the rocky nature of the coast. With hindsight it is possible to consider how things could have been done differently on 10 April 1968. But the fact is that both those on board the ship and those ashore did the best they could under perilous circumstances. Today, rescue authorities are better equipped with modern vehicles and rescue craft better suited to work in shallow waters. Ferries are better informed and equipped for dangerous situations. More importantly, if weather conditions are considered unsafe for the travelling public, they do not sail.

Many of those people directly involved on that day, either on board the *Wahine* or as a rescuer, still feel the trauma of the day's events. Some were left with permanent physical injuries, others had to cope with psychological effects. At that time people did not receive counselling after a traumatic event and were expected to just get on with their lives.

The experiences of 10 April were too much for some of the *Wahine* crew. The thought of going back to sea was terrifying, causing them to choose a life ashore. Deck boy Alan Windsor was determined to get back to sea as soon as possible as he felt it was the only way to get over his anxieties. The day after the disaster he joined the *Aramoana* as a deck boy. Standing on the rail ferry's deck as the ship went past the wreck of the *Wahine*, he felt thankful to be alive. He had nightmares for months afterwards, but is still at sea in 2003.

Captain Robertson returned to sea in September 1968 after the Inquiry when he joined the Union Company's trans-Tasman cargo ship *Kowhai*. He never commanded a passenger ferry again and spent his remaining years as master of a variety of cargo vessels. He was plagued by ill health and died of cancer in December 1973 at the age of 62.

Captain Galloway continued his career with the Wellington Harbour Board, becoming Harbour Master within a few months of the disaster. He remained in that position until his retirement in 1984. Harbour Pilot John Brown remained with the Harbour Board until the early 1970s when he left to join NZ Railways as master on one of their rail ferries. He remained there until 2001 when he retired as one of the Inter Island Line's senior masters.

Captain Cyril Sword who had been a Wellington Harbour Board harbour pilot since 1949 went on to become Deputy Harbour Master under Captain Galloway and retired in 1977. He died in 2002.

For Shirley Hick life was never the same again. Having suffered the tragic loss of Alma, for 22 years Shirley nursed her son Gordon, who died in October 1990 from injuries sustained on 10 April 1968. She looks back with pride on those years, as doctors had told her in

Gordon Hick was the final fatality of the disaster. Hick family collection

1968 that her baby would only survive for a matter of weeks. Due to Gordon's injuries, it was suggested he should be put in care. But Shirley insisted on nursing him for whatever time remained. She believes that the experiences of that tragic day, which affected both their lives forever, made her a stronger and better person and feels grateful for the years she was able to have Gordon in her life. Gordie, as she affectionately calls him, was the last fatality of that fateful day - 10 April 1968.

Those who Perished

Crew members

Hounsell, Howard Alexander   – Engine Room Hand.
Morrah, Christopher John   – Asst. Purser.
Murphy, George Vincent Austin   – Ist Class Asst. Steward.
Ross, John Spencer   – Pantryman.
Sayers, Laurie Angus   – Able Seaman – travelling in an unofficial capacity.
Symons, Samuel Stewart   – Motorman.
Udell, Robin Lester   – Officer Steward.

Another reminder of the Wahine is her main mast which has been restored and erected in Frank Kitts Park on the shore of Lambton Harbour, Wellington.

Passengers

Adamson, Ross James Arthur
Bear, Leah Edith
Beck, Margaret Morrison
Burton, Frederick
Clark, Anne Elizabeth
Cohen, Bertha
Cox, John Alfred
Doig, Cecil Noel
Duncan, Oswald Colin
Emmett, Margaret
Eriwata, Jessie Elizabeth
Evans, Olive Daisy
Folkard, Christobel Evelyn

Freitas, David Frank Errol
Goodman, Leslie Reginald
Gutschlag, Neil Douglas
Hick, Alma Anne (3 years)
Hickman, Henry Thomas
Hicks, Phillip Stephen (infant)
Hill, Maisie Mowat
Howard, Kathleen
Humphrey, John Baden
Jeffrey, Mary Agnes
Johnson, Colin Raymond (6 years)
Landreth, Gladys May
Marshall, Veda Catherine
McKay, Elizabeth Mary
McKee, Beatrice Ellen
Merton, Agnes Gertrude Stonyer
Metcalf, Anne Beatrice
Mitchell, Helen Patterson
O'Loughlin, Rose Annie
Page, Benjamin Joseph
Page, Elizabeth
Robertson, Wallace Allen
Rutland, Alfred Gould
Smith, Margaret Calder
Tabuteau, Eliza Mary
Townend, Brian Richard Churchill
Turner, Ethel May
Turner, Truby Lionel
Wasson, Cecil James
Williamson, Beryl Mary
Yee, Hong Yue

Archives of New Zealand collection

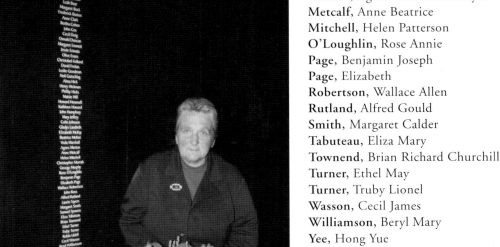

Shirley Hick on 10 April 2003 laying a wreath in the Wahine Gallery at the Museum of Wellington City & Sea.

A Tragedy Remembered

Above: *A view of the Wahine Memorial looking towards the Pencarrow Coast. The Inter-islander ferry* Arahura *can be seen headed out of the harbour on its way to Picton. The* Arahura *is approximately where the* Wahine *finally sank.*

The first time Shirley Hick (centre), met Billy Bell (left) and Jim Toulis (right), was when this photograph was taken at the Wahine Memorial for this book. For many years she had wondered who had rescued her son Gordon,

Captain John Brown and his crew on the pilot launch Tiakina *were the first vessel to respond to the distress calls on that terrible morning.*

Alan Windsor was a young seaman on the Wahine. *Despite the trauma of 10 April 1968, he was determined to continue his career at sea.*

Ray Whitham and many others worked in terrible conditions along the Pencarrow coast to save people from the sea.

58

All photographs taken at Seatoun Beach by Mark Coote

The Wahine anchor on the foreshore at Seatoun. The Memorial plaque plinth is attached to a section of anchor cable (chain) to one of the Wahine anchors. The anchor and cable are set out in such a way that they point towards the area where the Wahine foundered.

Rowan Hatch was the driving force in establishing a memorial dedicated to those lost in the Wahine disaster. After many meetings, and with the generous support of the Wellington City Council, sponsors and public donations, the Wahine Memorial was dedicated on 10th April 1993, twenty-five years after the disaster. Rowan also set up a small museum at the rear of his Seatoun pharmacy which attracted many visitors. When he sold the pharmacy the Wahine museum collection was transferred to the Museum of Wellington City & Sea. His efforts over the years have helped to keep the memory of the Wahine disaster alive in people's minds. The memorial was designed by the Wellington City Council landscape architect Peter Kundycki.

Shirley Hick and her son David Knight who was visiting from Melbourne, at the 35th anniversary commemorations.

Below: *On Thursday, 10 April 2003, the Museum of Wellington City & Sea commemorated the 35th anniversary of the sinking of the Wahine with a wreath laying ceremony and a series of public events. Hundreds of people joined with survivors and rescuers to mark the day. The central part of the museum was transformed for a concert by the Choir of the Wellington Cathedral of St Paul and members of the Central Band of the Royal New Zealand Airforce. The museum's large film screen featured a display of photographic images that depicted the drama of that tragic day.*

All photographs Mark Coote

Glossary of Terms

Abeam	Off to the side of a vessel
Aft	Towards the back of a vessel
Ahead	To go forward
Astern	To go backwards
Bosun	Leading Seaman
Bow	Front of the ship
Bridge	From where the ship is controlled
Coke	Fossil fuel (similar to coal)
Fore	Towards the front of a vessel
Forecastle/focísle	The deck area right at the front of the ship
Helm	Used to steer the ship
Knot	Used to indicate speed (e.g., 10 knots)
Leading lights	Lights used to guide ships in to a harbour
Lee	A more sheltered side of a ship
List	When a vessel leans to one side
Mess room	Area where crew eat their meals, relax and receive orders
Painter	Rope attached to lifeboat or raft
Poop deck	Situated right at the back of the ship
Port	The left side of the ship when facing forward, towards the bow of the ship
Providore	Stewards and catering staff
Roll-on roll-off	Able to drive on and off a ship
Starboard	The right side of the ship when facing forward, towards the bow of the ship
Stern	Back of the ship
T.E.V.	Turbo Electric Vessel
Ways	Timbers on which a new ship is launched in to the sea
Windlass	Machinery used to lower and lift the anchor

Bibliography

Newspapers:
Dominion
Evening Post

Court of Inquiry (1968)
T E V *Wahine*, Shipping Casualty, Report of Court of Inquiry. Government Printer, Wellington.

Books:
Ingram, C W N (1936), *New Zealand Shipwrecks*, 7th edition, Beckett Books, Auckland, 1990.
Lambert, Max and Hartley, Jim, *The Wahine Disaster*, A H & A W Reed, Wellington, 1969.

MacIntyre, David, Field, Michael & Quinn, Christine, *Cook's Wild Strait - The Interisland Story*, A H & A W Reed Ltd, Auckland, 1983.
McLauchlan, Gordon (ed), *The Line That Dared: A History of the Union Steam Ship Company*, Four Star Books, Auckland, 1987.
MacLean, Gavin, *Shipwrecks and Maritime Disasters*, Grantham House, Wellington, 1990.

Personal Accounts:
The following people were interviewed or discussed their experiences with the author: John Brown, Shirley Hick, Jim Toulis, Ray Whitham and Alan Windsor.

Author's Note

Frank Robinson was a steward on the *Wahine* when it foundered. His photographs of the events on the ship are a graphic record of the tragedy. When he abandoned ship in lifeboat S1, he lost extra rolls of film when the lifeboat capsized. He survived and continued serving at sea until he retired.

Special thanks to Mike Davies, Images Officer, University of Glamorgan, South Wales, United Kingdom, for the repair and restoration of the colour transparencies taken by David Hendy as he abandoned the *Wahine* on that fateful day.